Bedtime Stories For Kids (2 in 1): Daily Sleep Stories& Guided Meditations To Help Kids & Toddlers Fall Asleep, Wake Up Happy& Deepen Their Bond With Parents

By Mindfulness Meditations Made Easy

Bedtime Stories For Kids Daily Challenge: Daily Sleep Stories & Guided Meditation To Help Toddlers& Kids Fall Asleep Fast, Develop Mindfulness, Bond With Parents & Relax Deeply

By Mindfulness Meditations Made Easy

© Copyright 2020 - All rights reserved.

The content contained within this book may not be reproduced, duplicated or transmitted without direct written permission from the author or the publisher.

Under no circumstances will any blame or legal responsibility be held against the publisher, or author, for any damages, reparation, or monetary loss due to the information contained within this book; either directly or indirectly.

Legal Notice:

This book is copyright protected. This book is only for personal use. You cannot amend, distribute, sell, use, quote or paraphrase any part, or the content within this book, without the consent of the author or publisher.

Disclaimer Notice:

Please note the information contained within this document is for educational and entertainment purposes only. All effort has been executed to present accurate, up to date, and reliable, complete information. No warranties of any kind are declared or implied. Readers acknowledge that the author is not engaging in the rendering of legal, financial, medical or professional advice.

Contents

Nature Stories 1

Animal Stories 5

Barn Story 9

Protection Story 12

Flower Story 17

Security Story 21

Tree story 26

Trust Story 31

Water Fountain story 36

Creativity Story 40

River Story 44

Friendship Story 48

Mermaid story 53

Sea Travel Story 57

Whale Story 61

Dolphin story 65

Underwater Story 69

Rainbow story 73

Parents Story 77

Turtle Story 81

Long life story 85

Fire Story 89

Salamander Story 93

Jungle story 97

Monkey story 103

Rescue story 109

Bird story 111

Prince and Princess story 113

Fairytale story 116

Nature Stories

1378 words, 20 minutes

Once upon a time in a mystical land there lived a renowned Mother, Mataja, who was the keeper of the land and holder of the keys to the sacred castles.
She grew up on this land under a tree and she lived out in Nature the whole day and night. Her wonderful long hair in silver shone with experience and she was very wise.
Mataja could speak to the flowers and to the animals in respect and tolerance all the beings helped her and the people of this land.
When Mataja was outdoors, she collected herbs for medicine to bring this medicine to the needy. She was knowledgeable of all the flowers and trees, bees, animals and all you can know about nature.
When one was pregnant she knew exactly what to do, and which foods to supply as well as how the child would be delivered.

In the realms there also lived a king who was desiring a son, but He and His Queen were not able, until Mataja organized a walk in the forest with the king, to find the certain remedy for relief.

We can imagine a wild and lush forest that holds many green leaves, colourful fruits and flowers. The path into the forest is only accessible with the help of Mataja, who guides the King into the forest.

The flowers are greeting you, she smiles and gently stops, lets give these flowers attention and smile back. Smile. The flowers sense the attention and are happy that you are visiting.

The wonderful flowers in this mystical forest smell, and soothing scent arises at the tip of our nose. Inhale and Exhale, it is the best medicine. Where we start our life is with a simple breath. Flowers and other beings do the same. They all are breathing.
Breathing is the best and essential medicine. This is why this forest is sacred, because it breathes like we do.

Let's sit here and I think we have almost found what we are looking for. Mataja prepares a space for the King.

Meditate and I will be back with a handful of ingredients.
Then we start a fire to heat the water and to make tea. The sacred tea with the healing flowers will aid you.
Just sit here and feel at home, relax and be comfortable. Meditate and Breathe.

The King relaxes and feels pleasant in this Nature. Finally someone is taking care, he thinks. Suddenly, the trees bow to the king and start to talk: Welcome dear King, we are the mystical forest and here to greet you.

The king awakes from his meditation and gently smiles. I am happy to have you here and help me, we really want a son, and the queen is ready to receive one.

Mataja comes back with the basket full of herbs and flowers - she smiles, too, I am glad the forest welcomes you and bows. We are now ready to return to the Palast and bring the herbs to the Queen.

On a beautiful alley way the king looks into sky and wonders what the stars are saying, there must be a special occasion be happening in the heavens.

Mataja smiles and tells that every occassion is special, every being is one of a kind, and every single breath is unique.
Mataja, you are very wise and know Nature so well.

Nature is happy with me, because I am happy in nature. Lets bring these to the Queen and help her for her birth.
While the King and Mataja are on the Way home, the Queen is in her day dream and suddenly a white tiger comes into her dreams.

The Tiger announces, a Son will be born to you very soon, wait, be patient and constantly trust your kingdom.
The Queen is in wonder and startled looks outside the window. There the King and Mataja approach the Kingdom. Trust.

Trust me, bring these herbs to the Queen and let her bathe in the flowers. When you are ready, come outside for a small walk to the fire place, where I will be preparing the tea.
Mataja holds up the herbs and flowers for the kingdom and the Son shall be born.

As they bathe and wait, as the Nature is kind, so mercyful with a peaceful state of mind, the wonderful story will unwind, unfold and gracefully like the Queen bathing in flowers, dressed in garments of purity, the King and Queen shall be in Unity.

The Birds and Bees sing and hum, the echo of the flowers and trees enlightens the whole forest kingdom and beyond, the villages and towns, they All hear, a Son is born, a Son is born.
With flutes and harps, trumpets and drums, the festivity goes 9 months long.
Everyday they do the best for the Queen, serving her flowers and tea.

Once the Queen is happy, the kingdom will live in harmony.
So together they on the fire place, sharing a cup of unity.
Peace be with the forest, happiness be with the water, all come together at open fire, under the same sky.

The stars are out and shine oh so bright. There also moon reflecting this light. The fire burns and illuminates the happy faces of the party that celebrates with joy and dance.

The Nature is all happy too, as it watches us, the Happiness of us is also the happiness of All, Mataja says wisely. Let's prepare the blessing.

The oldest of the trees so wise and tall, old as no one ever could count, is now in presence to bestow a blessing for safety and security.

Everyone in the party is quiet and you can only hear the wind whistling in the dancing leaves of the tree, Maramta, the old and wise tree still wears fruit and shakes one of his branches.

With these fruits you shall feed your Son, so he might become a good heir with strength, beauty and grace he shall grow to be a wise man, Maramba smiles as gently as a tree can smile.

Beautiful world of speaking and smiling trees,
All happens under the night skies harmonies,
All is arranged in an order, with beauty and grace,
We look into the Moments space, there's a gentle face.
We find space, to take a deep breath and rest -
Let's wait for the best -
The blessing of the tree, the music to be free,

The dance, the music, the night liberate thee.

Mataja and Maramba bow in dignity and peace. The party is dissolved into eternity, the Waiting for the New born begins, and all prepare with joy and happiness. The Vision of the Queen became true, and the Son is born. With tender skin and lotus eyes, that shine like the sun, the baby is named, Samatura, the one that is always in balance and peace.

The Kingdom cheerful decorates everything in bright colours and the garden of the king is open for everyone to see, the first steps of a toddler, in grace and dignity.

Even sometimes when we fall, there is always the help of someone. Mother Nature holds us on this earth and blesses us with light and love. The trees provide the shadow, the water brings purity, fire light and in the night there the stars shine.

Imagine this world is all in the air, a possibility for everyone. As we are children of this earth, the presence under the sun, breathing the same air we are all in care. Nature is so rich and kind, everyone can find, a throne of the self. The body is here to help. Bringing us from one place to another, your hands, legs, head and heart all here for a reason.

Let's find the treasure of Joy that is in Nature, always and ever. Say Hello to the trees and smile. Be happy, that one is here.
Breathe and relax, all is friendly, as we are a friend to the earth, the Kingdom of Trees, Animals, Humans alike.

So we can imagine walking in the garden of the kingdom, together with the Son, the King and Queen, because we are all just a big family. See yourself happy and be happy, one is alive.
Smile, relax and have a good night.

Animal Stories

1564 words, 25 minutes

There once lived two monkeys in this mystical forest, Ernst and Herbert were very unusually clever and so smart, they went to the best universities, even sometimes people wonder how is this possible?

These monkeys had a teacher, a wise turtle named Kurma. This turtle lived just close to the mystical forest on the sea and hence the turtle holds time and space upwards, it just watches and observes the coming and going of the people. Kurma knows every little detail and habit, even someone scratching ones head out of uncertainty. The turtle observes the Nature all around and hence is very watchful and wise.

As the Monkey, Herbert and Ernst were playing, they wanted to show how clever they are and tried to play a game with the turtle. It is a musical game, where one is taking over the sound of the other one and adding more sounds to the circle. This game the two monkeys practice while the turtle played once and made so many sounds at the same moment, the monkeys were so in awe, they fell out of their rhythm and asked for guidance: How can you do so many things at once, just please accept us, and maybe you wise turtle can show us how you do the sounds of many ways.

Many ways I have travelled, Kurma says, across the land and see, long journeys come to ease, when I look these, you two are welcome and accepted, I may show you how.
So day and night the monkey sit besides the turtle and study with Kurma.

Sometimes, like us, they were just sitting in peace, just breathing and having a meditation.

Kurma guides this meditation and says, this meditation will bring harmony and well-being to your body and to your mind, that sits inside every cell of your body. Your body is made up of trillions of cells and every cell is alive and breathes.

Here, we can make all the body breathe, together, in and out, gently and slow, think about me, I am wise, gentle and so slow. Breathe in and out, gentle and slow.

Do you feel the relief and the calmness and peace?
Breathing into the nose, and breathing out of the nose, you can rest your eyes, half open, half closed. This will help to elevate any stress or disease, within the matter of a breath, there is the whole universe coming in and going out.

The breathing comes and goes, in and out, equally in and out, equally in and equally out again. Do you feel it?
Now focus on the nose-tip, and watch it, like opening of a river, the air streams in and out, it travels along your nose-tip, into the nose and to the heart.

Feel the rhythm of the heart, do you feel?
Feel the breathing streaming into the lungs and around the heart there is a feeling. Whatever this feeling may be, you are alive, breathing, and shall be happy. Be happy and content. Let the breathing move naturally and come to ease.

In the whole wide animal world I have met many teachers, but the real teacher sits within your heart. From your heart this inner teacher guides everything that is around you. Try to find this inner teacher within your heart. Breathe naturally and come to ease.

Once, Kurma explains to the monkeys, once I was meditating in the vast ocean and I noticed, no I need a good and calm place, then I meditated on the still lake and I noticed, no this lake is still but I can do better, and then I meditated upon a mountain. The monkeys look at each other, how can you walk upon a mountain?

The turtle Kurma smiles and says, easily I have found a guide, that carries me up there, so I asked the Eagle, please can you help me to the peak of this mountain? Of course, the eagle wanted to have me as lunch, but I offered my service, life-long, I shall bring you fresh sea fruits just let me be on this mountain for once.

In a lifetime of a turtle, Kurma laughs, who has thought to be on a mountain peak? Eventually the Eagle and I became friends and Elly the Eagle is also bringing me back down again. This is important, because sometimes I totally fall into deep meditation. It is almost like sleep, but I can move in my mind, which is the imagination to be wherever and whatever you like.

However, Elly did not forget me, and I am always thankful for her upliftment and for the chance to fly with an eagle once. Do you like to come on a flight or do you like to stay on your trees?

The monkeys look at each other, always together, now they were sure, only one can fly to the mountain with the eagle. But how can the monkeys know who is the one that can go on the adventure. Maybe Kurma knows a way to find the chosen one.

Kurma smiles, as I see it, you are both ready, but one is more ready than the other, find out who it is by finding Elly, who ever finds the eagle might go to the mountain peak with her.

The monkey start to seek out in the forest for the eagle, as one climbs up the tree, the other is sure, maybe I can make it onto the top alone. Without a word, both search the way, one calling from a tree, and the other one straight forward to the top.

There once were to monkeys, longing to go to the mountain peak, but only the way was clear from the birds eye and beak,
The sound of an Eagle echoes in the air, oh where oh where, I come to be named, Elly the Eagle world-renowed and famed, as I am not hungry for turtles, making Kurma my friend, he probably has some time to spend.

So Elly lands on the shore of the ocean to find Kurma who tells her about the two monkeys looking for a way to get to the top. The Eagle is laughing and finds that a monkeys belongs to the trees, but somewhere he sees, a monkey, on the way to the top.
Eagle Eyes so sharp see a monkey very smart, climbing with the help of a Yak, who knows the mountains without stop. They start to witness the other monkey calling from the tree, please dear Eagle help me!

The Turtle says, go before he starts to lose, let all be winners, and leave me behind. The story is here to unwind, as the Eagle flies to pick up Ernst from the tree, carrying him to the Peak. Herbert on the Yak, named Wadu, come with a scream WUHU! By the moment Herbert gets of the Yak to find a stand he mets the moment exactly where Ernst is here to land. Both monkeys on the peak, with the help of a friend, this has long no end, because the competition is off, as all realize where they are.

With a wonderful view, the panorama unfolds,
It is a blessed scene, one that Nature upholds.
The beauty of the moment, the wide horizon
And before, the golden sun.

Setting into the ocean, all realize, there is just one watching them all, Kurma, the turtle.
Laughing and laughing Kurma's laugh echoes to the peak - they all did it with grace and ease, one on a Yak, one with an Eagle, coming together, landing on the spot.

A while it takes, all look at each other, until Kurma calls; It's ok, you all are Winners! Come down and let's celebrate.
The Yak, The Eagle and the two monkeys choose the easy way down, to meet and party on the sunset beach.

Beautiful waves of bliss, and sunset stunning as always, the animals party a safe coming home. The night is there and the sky turns into beautiful rose, purple and blue, may this party be also one for you?
Together we sit and breathe, we celebrate life as it is. Together we almost reached the sky, but only now I wonder why.
Kurma helps us to see, everything is a possibility.
Maybe alone we are not strong, but together -
we can sing a harmonious song.

In harmony, one can be brave enough to have a friend, to take the chance and ask for help, may I have a hand?
At the moment you land, all is here to understand.
We are alive, thanks to the light, to the sky and the stars that shine oh so bright.

Let's rest and have a good, good night- Kurma holds the attention high; do you know what helps going to sleep? A good night story, but first we relax the body and mind. Slowly, breathe and gentle feel the air stream along the nose to your heart.

Blessed all beings be, and now let's have a Rest In Peace and harmony. Good night and maybe on another note I tell a story of a Yak, an Eagle and two monkeys climbing a rock.

All laugh and happily go for a good nights rest, so we All are a story, at ones best.

Sleep well.

Barn Story

<u>1283 words, 20 minutes</u>

Once there was a beautiful land rich in golden grains and fruits, all coming from the earth. The grass is fresh and green and the field forms around a river stream that provides the land with enough water flow. The farmer there is the One to know, and his name is Rich, like the land is rich, his name is too.
Rich knows everything about the land and he makes his barn open for everyone to visit. He believes in the everyone-is-welcome spirit.

Often there come volunteers to help and learn something that almost is forgotten; the art of making golden bread, from the seed to the bread, one who is ready can see the whole process. Rich is always enthusiastic about this bread and he also says, his bread is like medicine, once you have tasted this bread, you shall go well to bed. It's a bed bread - made from golden flour and fruits, lovely heated over the fire, crusty and crispy, well-done it can last for years and years to come, but the recipe comes from his Father. Richie Rich, his Father was a farmer, too but he was an expert for the Pie. Fruits for the pie, I still wonder why, he never got to be a millionaire, because his Pie is famous around the world. He would only care for the health of the family and the farm.

So, now we can make a journey on the barn, and what else is there to see? Yes, there is a whole cow family! We come along and Mooo, the cows awake, so lovely and kind, giving milk of all kind, sometimes we forget, the milk that is the best for bed.
The best its warm, and a little sweet, like this story. So no worry, all the animals are very well raised, as they have enough to do, Rich gives us a tour.

Here, he says, you can see the most wonderful indigenous cows, which are shy and serene, they love the golden hey and green field. Lets bring them out to the meadow, into the nature, into the grass. Every Cow has a name, Mula, Swaya, Mani, Ana, Vishu, Anja, Sahasra and they all hear very well.

When you call them, they hear you very attentively and Rich knows why. Cows all have a connection to the Milky Way, so all the sounds resonate in Harmony. This is Space-Cow science and I am actually training them to be the first cows in space. There is always astonishment in a cows face. When you look at them it is definitely wonderful to see a cow in space, but the training is more than an extraordinary phase. Sometimes Rich lets the Cows walk on cushions and feathers, so they prepare for anti-gravity.

In the summer time he lets them wear sun-glasses, cool cows, just to prepare. Of course one makes milk, Rich thinks about the first Space-Milk, but anyhow, the world isn't ready yet, but before we go to bed, a nice warm milk will make us fed, Rich smiles and shows us around the Barn to see the Pigs.

How does a pig make? Yes, this sound is unique as one knows pigs are the best at playing the nose trumpet. Actually Rich is conducting a symphony with the grunts and the moos. Moo Moo here, Grunt Grunt there. A barn is full and everywhere, you see a pig, you see a cow - oh WOW. There is a symphony.

The more we are on the land, the more the fresh air is here to tend. We breathe in and out, gentle and soft the fresh air streams along the nose, around the face and brings us new hope and space. We inhale and exhale, equally in and out again. The barn is still in peace and harmony, and we found a place in-midst the green field, watching the river stream, oh what a wonderful dream, of peace and serenity. There come 5 Chicken and one rooster to call for the evening. It is around that time, the chicken know and the rooster releases a loud: KIKERIKIII, strong and fierce all the chicken cackle and grin, with a victorious win, the farmer Rich starts to spin the weather rose, all animals must go, safe and sound to bed. First the Cows, blankets on top, with a warm and sweet good night, we say good night to all the cows: Good night Mula, good night Sways, good night Mani, Good night Ana, Good night Vishu, good night Anja, good nigh Sahasra, then we say good night to the Pigs, good night Pigs, then we say good night to the chickens and rooster, good night chicken and rooster.

All the beautiful animals live here rich in everyrhing, rich in space and good nights. The more we spend time on the barn, the more we notice the fresh air and calm peaceful evenings. Lets embrace once more, that we have a little oasis of serenity here with us. Lets give Rich and his Father a warm appreciative THANK YOU, lets say it innerly and bring our lips to smile. Lets smile and yawn, smile and relax. Just smile for awhile.

One can always come back to this barn, as this barn is within our heart and we can come here whenever we want. Is there a chance we can play with the cows or watch the pigs, or listen to the barn symphony with all the players, and when it is time, the rooster will let us know.

Now, let's relax the body, from head to toe, and find a comfortable position to rest. Imagine you sink into nice, comfortable hey, very dry and soft. See yourself resting, and feel how your head is relaxed. The forehead is eased and every tissue of your neck and shoulder is relaxed. The arms and hands are relaxing and comfortable.

We breathe and feel the relaxation spreading from the heart, to the belly and to the whole back. The whole upper body is relaxed and we breathe, equally in and equally out. We breathe and our thighs, legs, knees, ankles and feet relax, too. All our lower body is relaxed and light. The whole body is becoming lighter and lighter, with every breath we take, the body becomes lighter and lighter. There is more space and we feel the ease in the spine and every cell of the body. We can imagine how beautiful golden light spreads from the heart and and into every cell in the body. Golden light protects us and lets us feel warm and comfortable. The golden is soothing warm, nice and soothing. Every cell of the body is now in harmony and secure, fresh air is streaming into the nostrils and we are aware of the breath. Once more we give thanks to the Mother Land, to the Waters, the Sun and Moon, as well as all the beings.
A golden light expands now from our heart into the world and surrounds the whole world with a beautiful golden light of compassion and safety. We are happy and connected with all the beings. All beings are happy and safe, All beings are happy and safe, All beings are happy and safe.

Let the breathing air flow naturally and gently close your eyes and rest with compassion and kindness for all the beings.

May All beings be Happy and Safe,
May All beings be Happy and Safe,
May All beings be Happy and Safe.

Have a good rest and a soothing night, and if not, just imagine Cows flying in space towards the Milky Way.

Protection Story

<u>1636 words, 25 minutes</u>

Imagine there is a light, a beautiful light, that shines from within your heart. It is so bright and beautiful, it's around your whole body.

Breathe and feel the lightness throughout the whole body. See that light expanding with every breath. In and out, the breathing is equal and natural, the light expands and surrounds even the aura around you.

From within your heart there shines the source of this light and with every breath we illuminate our whole body, from the head, one can see the head glowing in a beautiful protective light, to the feet. With every breath the light travels throughout the body.

We start from the crown of our head, there is a the light slowly sinking into the face. We breathe and with every breath, the light sinks lower and lower into area of the eyes. Our eyes and all the muscles around the eyes are illuminated with protective, healing light.

Just focus on the breathing and let the light sink into the ears, the cheeks and jaw. All the little tissues and membranes are equally illuminated, around the nose, on the jaw, and inside off the head, where the nose meets the mouth. We focus on this point, where the nose meets the mouth and clearly sense our breathing. We can even hear the breath coming in and going out again. It is a constant stream of energy that comes with the air, and the sound is clear and soothing.

One can find comfort in the sound of the breath and know there is a light, a life protection from within and around us.

The Life Breath is everyones mandatory need.and we can connect with this friend our whole life. It is always there for us. Lets breathe again and feel how mandatory and friendly the life air is.

See the focus where the nose and mouth meet.and sense the air coming into the nostrils and going out again. It is a constant Hello, Breath. Goodbye Breath. Always and ever coming and going. We are just witnessing this process, this endless stream and ensure everything is smooth and equal.

Equally in and out again, the protective light shines within our whole head and a feeling of peace and protection spreads around the face. We can smile and ease into the breath. Maybe sigh or yawn, whatever feels now fine with you.

Also note any sensation, whatever it is, warmth, cold, vibrating, tickling, throbbing, pulsing, any sensation is possible, and whatever comes, we keep on breathing.

We see the breath traveling into our nostrils and down the throat into the lungs. From our head and our heart the protective light also illuminates the throat and neck area. Along the spine the protective light shines in every cell from the head, to the throat, to the middle of the body.

Here the light sinks further down with the breath and we include as many parts as possible, like the shoulders and arms, elbows, wrists and hands. All are surrounded with protective light. We can open our hands to the sky and see how the light illuminates now every cell, even the finger tips.

Lets put our hands into our middle, onto the belly and feel into the body. Protective light is spreading from the hands and from the heart into the belly and around the whole lower body. The healing light of protection axpands and brings peace and ease.

We breathe and with every breath the light sinks further down the spine, from the belly to the hips, into the root of the spine. Here we relax and find that the healing light of protection is welcome to also illuminate our thighs, knees, legs, ankles and feet. The healing light of protection even shines into the smallest parts of the tippy toes and brings peace and relaxation.

From the tippy toes we can come upwards, according to our breath we can travel with the awareness, the light of protection up the legs, to the bottom of the spine and again, slowly up the spine to the heart. Here, in the heart we hold this healing light of protection and let it blossom like a flower.

With every breath, each and every pedal of this wonderful flower of light expands from the heart and shines throughout the whole body. The whole flower of light is now really beautiful and blossomed. We can imagine we are meeting a friend, and we can bring this flower as a present to the heart of this friend.

Let's smile and innerly say: Here, this is the light of my heart, may it protect and bring you peace.
You can repeat this prayer and see your friend kindly accepting it.

Here, this is the flower of my heart, may it protect and bring you peace.
Here, this is the flower of my heart, may it protect and bring you peace.
Here, this is the flower of my heart, may it protect and bring you peace.

By saying this we give meaning to the flower and to the light, therefore one knows what this light intends to do.
Protection and Peace is now upon us and we can see the whole body of ours and our friend be illuminated.

By breathing we uphold the light, by breathing we maintain the luminosity.

Whenever we are in a hurry, we can also call this protective light and ask for healing light of protection. Please Light, Protect me, and give me shelter of Peace. The healing light is like the breathing always with us, when we are aware of it, it comes into presence.

In our imagination lets wander around our home and in the garden to maintain this healing light. Just breathe and feel the connection to the sunlight. See how the light of protection and the sun light are one and the same.

See the trees and the grass, and know all this is grown from the sunlight, one with the light of protection. See the sky and the endless horizon and know, your inner voice can always call for the light of protection.

May All beings be in protection and Peace,
May All find relaxation and ease.
May All have a life of light and love.
May All live in Peace and Harmony,
May All join the Unity.

For a good nights sleep this protective light can bring us from the unsafe shores of darkness to the beautiful shores of the light kingdom.

Find yourself comfortable and relaxed, you are now safe and in protection. We are sailing over the ocean of darkness, but without any fear, we have friends, teachers, and guides of light on our side.

They know how to steer the ship into the waves, sailing with the wind, even the mermaids are helping us for good fortune and protection. Even the Fish and the Turtles are helping us for good. Also the wind and water, are good to us, soothing when there is too much going on, and there is the sun for direction, in which way to go.
We are in midst the sea, and the elements, as well as all the passengers are chanting a song of protection and good will.

Let's all trust on the travel,
Across the land and sea,
Lets unite people and everyone in balance and harmony.

Look, there might be a long way in front of us,
All we essentially need to do, is to trust & Breathe.
Let's See, together we may live in Harmony.

When there comes a time of sorrow,
We may speak it out and ask: What is going on?
Let's come to shore and find a place of Harmony.

Let's imagine the vessel finds a land, taking on the ropes to the harbour and taking care of all the passengers including one Self. We are safe to shore guided over the sea of ignorance, into the land we finally find peace, protection and harmony.

Let's see and imagine, all there is. The people are smiling and inviting us to come along. Let's celebrate the arrival and say good bye to the day. As the vessel takes off into the sunset, it slowly gets cooler and find a cozy place for the night, are we alright?

Still breathing, into the nostrils and into the heart, the protective light of healing and harmony is illuminating our whole being and we find shelter, with our friends and family.

Let's sing and dance together for good joy and celebration to be healthy and well.
Let's chant a simple Mantra for Guidance and Protection of the whole world.

I am the light of the world,
I am the light of the world,
I am, I am, I am the light of the world.

You are the light of the world,
You are the light of the world,
You are, You are, You are the Light of the world.

We are the light of the world,
We are the light of the World,
We are, We are, We are the light of the world.
The sing-song enchants and brings light to the moment, even going to bed, we can shine our light to be safe and sound.
Feel the breathing slowly relaxing and smoothly coming in and going out. Let's once more give thanks to the Light, the sun and moon, as well as all the people that shine their light of attention to Us.

Let's gently close our eyes and find our inner paradise, on the safe shores of protection and harmony.
Let's smile and be happy,
Have a deep breath and let yourself sink into the night,
may there always be protection and light.
Have a good, good night.
May there always be light.

Flower Story

<u>1413 words - 20 minutes</u>

Once upon time in a magical land, where kings and queens lived together in peace and unity, everyday was a festival. A festival of Life, where everyone came together to dance, sing and appreciate the presence of life.

The land gave many fruits and flowers, and therefore the people of the kingdom spend much time outside. On the land side, there was was a simple flower lady who offered her services for the king to maintain collecting flowers for all the festivities. By that she could contribute to the whole kingdom and make enough for a living.

Together with her maids she visits the palast every day to bring the full flower baskets to the ceremonies, where they are first offered to the holy Altar. It is always very early in the morning, there takes a ceremony place that is so beautiful and enchanting that it many thousand people in and lives on to this day.

Sometimes the flower ladies are unnoticed, but the flowers are an essential part of the whole process.

We bring flowers to the priests and they offer them with water and milk to the altar, then we have a festivity of chanting and dancing and thanking for all the gifts that Mother Earth provides us in many folds. The flower lady smiles, with a flowery presence, she loves the attention by the Kingdom who chose her to bring light on the whole ceremony.

Flowers are also very talkative and healing, we can go into the garden and ask a flower what kind of weather will be. Just sit there and breathe, wait and the flower will let you know. So kind and fine, the flowers are subtle and beautiful in nature, just choosing to be fragrant and graceful.

We can also scent a flower and compliment one another with these smells and colours. On likes to go to bed, well then we can choose flowers that are relieving and good for a night, however we are still in the kingdom celebrating so we choose flowers with bright colours and light scents.

The flower lady smiles and starts to dance a little from left to right, Devi is her name and she serves with flowers from her childhood.
You know, everything is changing much, however all the ways we do things are still remaining the same. Even the flowers change a little, yet they remain always one with us, as the ways we do things never change, it is like breathing.

Breathing flowers and dancing in a flower field is my favorite activity, she laughs and grins at us. Come let's go for a walk and I show you my favorite place. It is by a beautiful source, leading into a spring, where the grass is lush and green, the soil holds rich minerals that make the flowers be bright and beautiful - let's go.

So we walk together with Devi through the fields and meadows, around the forests and beside the stream we hear the lush sound of the waters, that lead us to the source. Oh smell, these are my favorite flowers, very special and fine in nature, they are so tender, they hear every word I say. Let's get closer and watch the flowers and ask them kindly for a blessing.

We come closer and see the flowers from a close, with magnificent colours and stunning forms they interact and show the Grace of Creation. We see different ones, red, and purple flowers that are waiting and dancing in the wind. As soon as we see them, we inhale and see, how the flower pedals are slowly opening and showing their inner beauty.

The inner beauty shines with kindness and an unforgettable smell that instantly relieves any disease. We become so attracted, we like to get closer, however there are so many more flowers, it is a whole ocean of flowers, in colours blue and light blue we find flowers that are fine and small, we find gross and solid ones, we find also flowers that have scents that attract butterflies.

There is one in light rose and one in yellow with beautiful punctuation and symbols on the wings, we also see them land inside a flower and disappearing for a moment. It takes a while, but then the butterfly happily flies out and searches for a playmate.

As we sit and watch the butterfly find another butterfly to play, we observe how slowly the rain comes in. A warm and soothing rain covers our head and skin. We feel a rain drop running down our cheeks and along our chin.

The flower lady invites us to dance and play in the rain, as it is like music, we celebrate the serene scene with joy and happiness. Together with the butterflies we dance and sing along to the song of the rain.

It is the rain song, come and sing along, to that beautiful song, come let's sing along.
May all beings be like flowers harmless and kind
With a beautiful smell with the wonderful taste of the divine
Heartily enjoy the colors and the scents,
In nature it is always good to spend
Life is beautiful as is it is - let's pray
So shall it be for every time and day
Let's connect Ourselves to the good way.
Every drop of rain feels so fine and okay.
I might be happy, and in harmony,
With the flowers, the rain, the soil and sun,
I feel like life is blooming and just has begun.

Every breath one takes there Is possibilty to awake
Let's enjoy the travel and give the night a chance,
Prepare with simple breathing and just feel fine and ok.
Like you are laying in a bed of flowers, so soft and tender you sink in, and with every breath there is more space to relax, let's relax into the breath to sink more and more into the bed of flowers. The wonderful feeling holds on and one listens to the breathing, slow and rhythmic in harmony with the body and mind.
Keep the breathing equal and fine and try not to think to much, just enjoy the bed of flowers, Let yourself sink and feel how the body is becoming lighter and lighter, Like a butterfly we become smaller and smaller, we can sense the lightness of the body which transforms into a small, tiny speck of light. We are now this light and it is so light you can be as light as light itself.
Feel the ease and surround yourself with the comfort of the night. Slowly we sense the breathing again and nice fresh air flows into the body, and the light returns back to the bed of flowers.
One is there, just breathing and we invite one of our best friends to come along into the beautiful flower garden with us, there we can roam and play for a while until we are again coming back to our selves.

Just imagine the free space and endless lush field in your imagery flower garden, where a bed of flowers and a friend always wait for you, go and enjoy the space.

When there is the moment to come back, we reconnect with the body and breathe again. The breath is the bridge between the imagery world and the body.

Just breathe and now the breath is always with you, like a good friend, that comes along on a journey to travel with you. Patiently and persistently breathe and feel the ease.

With every breath the lightness within the body spreads from the heart, the center of light, into the whole body. Breathing in and out, equally, will bring balance to the whole body and there we find the space to relax and imagine.

It is like the soil,
The breath,
Like the rain that comes,
The in and out,
It is the flower that grows,
Oh, the Nature knows.
The rhythm equal and steady,
Are you ready?

Say goodbye to the flower lady and follow along to have a nice soothing sleep on your flower bed.

The lady further comes back with a flower garland, beautifully decorated and made of the most fragrant colours of your favorite flowers, coming just to you with a smile, what a present! We smile and keep on the smile into our soothing night, alright.

Let's rest, relax, breathe through and wish for a good, good night.

Security Story

<u>1667 words, 25 minutes</u>

There is a space within the universe where we are all safe and sound. It is the heart of the Absolute Truth, the well-wisher of all beings, as it is the location of the Highest Truth, the one living there is the creator of this universe, with many names and faces, this person gives us shelter in form of a lotus flower.

This Lotus flower is the protection that sits within everyone's heart.

This story my Father always told me, the son Samatura says, smiling and having a glance into the sky, but where is security in the outside world? When I feel insecure, what can I do?

Samatura is now not a little child anymore, he can think and be aware, of certainty and uncertainty. Like us, he knows, there are dangers in the world, but he is brave enough to live a life.

He breathes through and follows the river into the forest where his teacher is situated. Sandapa will know, he is a wise man and contributes to the wellbeing of all his disciples and students, but he is more encouraged to share his message of security and peaceful living in this world.

The question of Samatura still roams in his head, where there is security in me, there also must be security within every one.

Let's prepare to meet Sandapa, who usually sits under a tree in the forest and writes his scriptures and ancient texts. He is living in the forest for his whole life and never had any fight. Living in security and peace he teaches this message for everyone, especially for the Son of the Kingdom who one day will remain in position to lead the kingdom to many more generations.

Sandapa awaits the young disciple and son of the Kingdom with a smile. He is very lean and tall, with bright eyes and tender cheeks, his hear is white and he sits under a tree.

I see, you are walking alone from the kingdom, do you think you are free? Bring a friend to come along with you, therefore security will come true. Sandapa grins and knows all the questions by his disciple. Yet, he invites him to sit for a meditation and we all can join.

Let's find a comfortable position, where we are align with the ground and with the sky. Come to ease in that position and gently close your eyes. Let it be like a window opening for the holy altar.

There, on this altar you see many beautiful deities and pictures of saints, like great masters and mystical beings. See yourself sitting in this holy place and find ease, watching the candle lights and smelling the inscence, so fragrant and nice, the whole room is filled with joy and happiness. It is secure and safe, therefore we don't have to worry about anything. Just breathe, equally in and out, see the air flowing in regularly, and constant, and see it flowing out, regular and constant.

One is safe, to be breathing means to be in the security of life. Here in the body, we are safe, here in the sacred room we are safe, here with a guide and teacher we are safe. Feel the shelter and open your heart, like a lotus flower. Let this lotus flower bloom and see every petal of this lotus flower adjust to the light.

The light shines from your heart and illuminates the room, the petals of the lotus flower open and one is surrounded by this lotus flower light.

Did you know, that lotus flowers even grow in the deepest swamps, where there is hardly pure water and light? Yet, the lotus flower remains unspoiled and graceful in-midst this nature.

Let's go for a soothing and mild walk down the forest lane to find a swamp with many lotuses. There we see the trees opening up a way for Us, the alley leads straight to a little muddy swamp, where we find a wooden floor. Let's wait here and see the flowers in the distance.

With shimmering silver and purple the petals of the lotuses surround the yellow golden middle, the stigma. It is a splendid wonder to look at, but how can the lotus flower feel safe in this swamp, so dark and moist?

It is a wonderful question, let's explore the answer and ask the Lotus flower, Sandapa smiles and plugs a lotus flower, which he will offer to the sacred altar in the room. He knows the answer already but he promises us to bring this lotus flower into a safe place, where he gives it to the other offerings like fruits and milk to the deities.

While we return, the Lotus flower starts to speak and gives us many interesting answers to our questions.
In a subtle and clear voice the purple-golden Lotus says:
I am secure, when I am within me, as the sun light comes, I open up. I trust, the sunlight is my benefactor bringing me growth.
As the Lotus explains the ways to come to a place of security we share a human place of security we call home, this home is the place where we find community and joy in the things we do, together with our loved-ones, we live here, work, study and find shelter.

Samatura is obliged and puts this beautiful lotus flower on his head, I will bring this back to my father, so I can tell him everything about, what I learnt today with you. Thank you, kindly accept my humble obeisances. Samatura bows in reverence and walks on with a lotus flower on his head.

In a beautiful kingdom, that longed to be at peace,
We can explore and walk around the forest at ease.
There also is a teacher and when we kindly ask, please.

Give us an answer to our questions, bring us release,
The teacher may illuminate the darkness into light.
As long as there is no fight, we are alright.
Let's enjoy this little bit of life, feel and shine bright.
Even, when we have to say goodbye the day and hello to the night.

As always the day ends, in every wonderful kingdom, and eventually there comes the night. In this Kingdom it is tradition to have a safe and sound ceremony, with oil lamps, and a concert. Beautiful and serene at the same time, the students of Sandapa, as well as the Son of the King, Samatura, are joining the good night ceremony with lights and chants.

Samatura chants:

May all beings be at peace,
May all beings find their ease,
Shall all live in harmony,
Peace, Love and Unity.

The trees are watching the stars, the birds are tweeting their songs, together with the stars that illuminate the night, today there shines a special light, it is a full moon show, with special honor to all the Mothers and Teachers.

There, Mother Nature becomes a special thanks and appreciation, there also all the teachers are handed wonderful flower garlands and presents for their service.

All fits together under the beautiful night sky, the mild wind blows into the trees, and makes the leaves start to dance. There is a chance we see Mataja making a sacred fire, one can sit and see the sacred procession of inscence and milk, with flowers and oil lamps, we can also see the holy rivers and streams, that are being honored and everyone from the kingdom joins together in harmony.

We feel safe, and sound on this night.
We can breathe safety and protection. With every inhale there comes safety and with every exhale we let go the uncertainty.
We inhale security, and let go uncertainty with the exhale.
Breathe and feel the security coming to you, and the uncertainty leaving you, more and more we relax and find space to smile.
Let's be happy and celebrate life as it is. Even in this night there certainty, tomorrow the sun will rise, as always, we give thanks to our Mothers and Teachers that help us on our path and we thank Mother Earth for Life.

We now relax our body, with every breath, there comes upon relaxation, of the body, and mind. We are relaxing the head, the head is relaxed, breathe equally in and out, now relax the neck and throat, the neck and throat shall relax, we breathe in and out.
Now let's relax the shoulders and arms, elbows, palms and fingertips, breathing in and out, the shoulders, arms, elbows, palms and finger tips relax.
We shall relax the chest and upper body, inhaling and exhale, we do so. We shall relax the belly and lower back, inhaling and letting go with the exhalation. The whole of the upper body is now relaxed.

Now breathe and relax the thighs, legs, knees, ankles, feet and tippy toes, all the parts of lower body relax with the next inhale and exhale the whole body is relaxed.

Now we calm our thoughts, as we imagine a beautiful light giving us protection and security, this light fulfills our heart and blossoms like a wonderful lotus flower.

This Lotus flower shines in the most wonderful colours and protects us. The light reaches every parts of the body, every cell and we see ourselves in this light, engulfed and surrounded with a healing light of security.

Put your palms together and feel the harmony and security. Feel good and let the breathing be natural. Like a lotus flower, you can now open your hands and bring them to your lotus eyes. Surround your eyes with the healing energy of the hands and let your eyes bathe in the palms of your hands. Breathe, equally in and out. Breathe, just naturally.

Maybe sigh, or massage your head, around the eyes and your jaw to feel totally fine. All is now safe and sound, with a smile we are ready for a good, good night.

Rest, and relax completely.

Tree story

<u>1374 words, 20 minutes</u>

In this mighty Kingdom, once upon a time, there lived the oldest and wisest trees in the world. These trees were so rooted, that no one could shake them, as these trees were holding onto the ground, no one could ever rip them out, no giant, no dragon, no king, nor queen, but they all know, the wonderful humbleness of a tree.

So humble and kind, the tree doesn't care, about all this, the tree is not winning any price, but the honor and respect of all human kind. Even the wind, sometimes tries, but hardly comes to terms with this forest kingdom, where the trees hold onto their roots.

We have to appreciate the tradition and the groundedness of these wonderful ancient beings, that have stood the test of time, further trees evolved with us, and before us, so they know everything about the earths history.

Once in a lifetime of a tree, he has to hold space for birds and humans alike to have a nest. Sometimes, big birds are bringing many sticks and branches to the crown of the tree, to build a nest.
This nest then, is a place for the children, the baby birds and offsprings to gain experience and to grow up. When a bird family is ready, they move into another place, but this can take a long while.

Same with the people of the kingdom who want to live at the feet of the wonderful trees, and therefore sometimes build little huts on the ground to find shelter and security in the woods of this kingdom.

Trees are often so humble, they accept everything that other beings bring to them, even their saws and nails, trees are that tolerant, however one shall treat a tree, like oneself treats a friend.

The friendliness of the trees surely comes back in for of wisdom and inspiration, as the tree breathes out the air, we breathe in and likewise the other way around, we breathe out, the air, that the trees breathes in.

The circle of air, flowing from the lungs of the person, to the plant and other way around is the circle of life. We can feel this, breathing in and breathing out, feeling safety and protection, just knowing the shelter of the trees will be there.
Trees are also very much delighted by our presence, as we come to a tree, we can bow down and greet the tree with happiness and joy. The tree knows, and feels tine with that.

When we humans bring a light or a candle, we have to be very careful, because the tree knows, that this can also hurt us, and of course, it is like the sun light, we are all connected.

So one day, Samatura went into the forest. However, this time he left his kingdom not alone, but he brought a group of friends, that all wanted to meet his teacher, yet the teacher was not sitting as usual under that tree. He must have been for a walk.

So the group around Samatura was curious and wanted to know, what to do in the forest. As we all like to roam and play in the forest, it was unlike that Samatura wanted everyone to sit by the tree and to listen.

Therefore we all sit, with the tree, and however meditating like the tree.

So find a comfortable position and imagine your spine. You see the spine, vertebrae for vertebrae and there is also a root, imagine, the root coming from the lowest bottom of the spine and spreading throughout the soil, into the layers of the ground.
That ground then is the fundament for our balance.
So we breathe, and breathe in the balance. Equally in and out,
Balanced breath, equally in and out.
All in harmony and balance, the breathing flows naturally and the body is align with all the elements. As the spine is straight, we are relaxing our jaw and head. We can let go of any tension, to relax and ease, into a smile.

Breathe and smile, gently.
Breathe and be in balance.
Like the roots of a tree, we find steadiness in the ground.
And we can also tone a sound, that helps us to relax.
Lets open our mouth, wide and full, on AHHH, hold the sound as long as possible.
AHHHH

Now breathe again and find the balance and harmony, in the ground, and of course we can tone another sound.

This time for our heart, the Sound goes UHHHH, very mild and long, we can tone this once more, UUHHHH and there you connect to your heart and now lets embrace the smile, lets connect to our head with HUMMMM, long and gently, sound HUMMMMM. These three sounds, AHHH, UHHH, HUMMM are the essential building blocks of life

Like a tree has a seed, that's the AAH, it also has a stem, that's the UHH, and of course it has a crown and that's the HUMMM.

All together these three sounds AUM give the primal sound, a wonderful invention.

The trees are mostly silent, but they can understand all the sounds of the universe, therefore we always have to be conscious what we say in our environment, as we are peaceful, breathing and meditating, the environment, the trees and all the other beings are very happy with us.

Of course we can smile and find our happiness within our heart. There, a wonderful lotus flower blossoms and we see, that everyone's lotus flower is the same, yet different.

Everyone is breathing the air, yet we are all different from the inside.

All the trees are of the same structure, yet, every tree is one of a kind. Isn't that beautiful?

Let's relax and find out how the trees are embracing the night.

A tree doesn't really need to close the eyes to sleep, yet knows exactly when the sun is setting, therefore around this time, the tree gives everything into the atmosphere, to celebrate and cheer the great gift of life.

Sometimes, a lot of flowers are coming from a tree, sometimes, the tree dances in the wind to find expression, and sometimes the fruits of a tree are growing from just a little seed.

One seed has all the information a tree needs to live on for thousands of years, and even in the nights, the trees are growing upwards and downwards, isn't that interesting?

As all the beings, like the trees are part of this world, we are also growing in the night, yet, we have to be sure, that we are relaxed and ready for the upcoming night. Therefore the trees prepared a nice soothing song for the upcoming good night.

It is again, around that time, where everything sets, from the shine, of the sun, to the son, of a kingdom divine. Please, enjoy the moment, and breathe, like we are here together to live.

Enjoy the moment and breathe,
The air comes in and out,
There is so much doubt,
But leave it all behind,
Be sure and one shall find,
That there is more to the dark,
That there is always a spark,
That ignites the wisdom of life.

Even thought we respect the light,
We know, it must be night,
Whenever we are in sight,
we arrange to be alright,
With a song, that goes all night long.

Sing it and feel it in the breath.
Sing it and feel it in the air,
Breathe and be enjoying the now.
Everything is in care, just trust, just trust.
There is no more, do's or must.
Just relax and keep the breath,
Feel the peace and the ease.

Root yourself to the ground,
And hear the beautiful sound.
It is the air, in the space,
Now imagine a face,
Let it be kind and smile,
Hold it on for a while,
Enjoy the sight,
For a good, good night.

In the moment we listen to the trees, we are also listening to our selves, conscious and wise, we are all rooted on the same earth.
Be kind and bring your friends, to this wonderful kingdom of peace and harmony.
Enjoy every bit of it.
Rest and sleep well.

Trust Story

<u>1531 words, 20 minutes</u>

Trust is the true essence of relationship. Sometimes we go blind when so in love, that we trust the world in a child-like feeling as being in the Mothers womb.

Samatura was traveling to the forest with a friend who suddenly asks to stand still and wait. I hear something. It is like a tree is talking to me. Yes, this can happen in the middle of the forest, there might be a tree. Waiting and holding for a breath, Samatura just trusts his friend in curiosity and then suddenly he hears it, too.

There is a voice whispering. Trust me, there is a storm coming, a big thunder rolling in, you better have a shelter, somewhere in the kingdom, trust me, a storm is coming.

Samatura and his friend are looking at each other and agree, to trust the tree. Hey, we are free, but being pulled away by a storm, we can see, is better to come inside and wait it out.

Very protected and safe the home of the palast is waiting for them. Both of the young boys are walking down the wild forest lanes, looking into the distant lands. Somehow, Samatura feels now, what the tree was saying, the weather is changing, even though they still see people walking and playing on the streets.

Trust the tree and worry for your friend and yourself, as everyone worries for the close one and oneself, everyone is in care. Let's find the way back to the kingdom's garden.

There are always some signs that a storm or weather is coming up, and there we can learn something here. There are flowers, called the weather flowers, that instinctively close their petals as soon as something comes up. Same with weather trees, weather frogs and weather people, that intuitively know what is going to happen.

Just trust, and you will be alright,
Even when there is no storm in sight,
Please trust the beings around you,
As one says it honestly it sounds true.

Truth and trust ring a bell,
Let's all trust and be well.
There is intuition in every cell,
One might be the one to tell.

So trust yourself and find a way,
Speak it out, and be the One to say,
Let's change, let's awake and hey,
There might be another beautiful day.

So Samatura and his friend trusted the tree and thank god they arrive early in the kings Palais where everyone wondered where have you been. Oh what a surprise and the first drops come down, thanks to the tree, we made it early. Thanks to the tree?

Yes, we heard the tree speak, so subtle and fine he whispers, there might be a storm, better come home, better go now. There might be a storm, trust. And we trusted ourselves and the tree, so kind and humble bowed to thee.

Now, we are happy, waiting for the storm in security. Possibly, there is a chance that we might be watching this storm for days on end, but that's life in protection and with a friend.

Samaturas Friend smiles and gives a cheerful song from his lips.

There once was a kingdom, no storm could shake, just the right time to awake and we find ourselves in the midst of the mystical forest, where trees can talk and animals can walk.
Every day here is a festival, we celebrate the sensations of Mother Nature, the endless changes, that come and go.

Let's sit with your teacher and meditate.

Also in the Kings palast there are many rooms for once in a while the teacher comes by to read and study the scriptures with the young boys from the kingdom, already so brave and wise, they know nature, but they also shall know the divine.

There is Life in every being, the teacher says, there is life in every cell. Therefore we can sense all the body with just a thought.

Now, instantly, I can know how my little toe is doing, just by thinking of this part of the body.
There is intelligence in the whole body. Let's try.

Bring yourself to ease and breathe. Do you feel your tippy toes? Breathe and relax, there is awareness, so energy in the little toe, the first toe, the second toe, the third toe and the fourth toe. Do you see and feel? Be aware, that energy is now filling the space in your feet and breathing makes it happen.

Breathe and feel again, your toes are alive and relaxed. Now feel your whole feet- Be aware of the energy at the feet. Be aware of the ankle and of the whole leg. Now of the thigh, the root of the spine and the whole spine. Breathe and feel into the body, now your whole lower body is relaxed and filled with awareness. Sense the trust and the security, be aware of the belly and now imagine you find shelter in a deep, deep cave made of rose crystals.

Imagine walking into this crystal cave of light and glowing crystal quartz in rose. One can see the reflection and the beautiful splendor of the rose, it is a whole cave with nice rose colored walls, all surrounding you. One finds a place in the crystal cave to sense the stability and protection. Just trust and feel safe.

The whole of your body is in union with the awareness and we start to be breathing slower and slower, we are becoming finer and finer and with every breath we are becoming lighter and lighter. Our whole upper body is now filled with peaceful and radiant light. From the belly it radiates to all the parts of the body. The chest is filled with awareness and we feel the chest. There is a room, where we meet our friend, and kindly greet our friend with a smile. Smile and feel the friendship eternally from the heart. The whole heart and the upper body are now illuminated with the light of friendship.

Just breathe and feel the sensations coming and going, sense the air and know every storm also might pass. The air comes and goes again. All is coming and going, but we are here, right now in safety and peace. Now relax your head with the light of peace. Peace be with every part of the head and jaw. All is illuminated in peaceful light of relaxation.

The whole head relaxes and we find absolute serenity in the breath. Breathing equally in and out, all is in care, all is fine and we find the ease.

The Storm is outside and is now noticeable as the two boys thank each other and the teacher for the serenity.

Let's together speak a prayer for the kingdom and for the whole world.

May all beings in this kingdom and the whole world be happy and at peace.
May all beings be at peace and happy.
May we all find absolute serenity.
May there be trust and happiness all around,
May we find the inner voice that guides us,
Torwards peace, love and unity.

Trust starts with trusting one self. This trust to oneself comes from the knowledge who we are and what really is. With meditation, says the teacher, we can learn how life really is.
It is like the storm sometimes, unknown, behind the clouds, and as it is coming, sometimes in the air, and then eventually passing away again.

Thank you, dear teacher, Samatura and his friend Dandilion are happy that they are inside now, whereas the storm is breaking down and it might take awhile for the storm to ease and rest again, but it is almost night and the thoughts are easing with a glass of warm cow milk and they talk about the good adventures that they experienced in the forest.

Do you remember taking this bow and sticks into the forest and you shot this apple off my head, precisely, like always? It was just a practice shot from very close, next time we do it, I have to be 3 kilometers away, not 2. Yes, maybe the tree can help us prepare, as I know they are very calm and steady.

I love these trees, says Samatura with a smile, they give me so much space to play, I might never grow up around a forest tree like that. That's the way, agrees his friend. Trust your inner Child, it might be the most precious livelihood one has.

Let's enjoy the milk and head to bed. Yes, we are all calming down and dreams may come true. All is in care and the boys from the kingdom are willing to maybe one day find a unicorn, as there are many mysteries in this forest, there also is a story of a unicorn, but that might rest for another time. Now, we prepare for sleep with a trusting light, that fully surrounds our body for good sleep. From head to toe, and from toe to head. Feel and relax. Now the whole body is relaxed. Ease in and find your sleep. Sleep well.

Water Fountain story

<u>1518 Words, 25 minutes</u>

Once upon a time there was a market place with a wonderful water fountain in the midst of it. The water fountain was known to heal and protect the masses from diseases and cure old age and fogetfulness. This water fountain never stopped to talk, as it springs and springs, water comes from its mouth, deep from the earth. In the well there are many coins for good fortune and the well is always visited even into the night.
The market place did not know any rest, it was just as busy as always and good business one was making here for sure, as there are so many people attracted to this spring the water flows and so business flows. One day, there came the king into town with all his consulates and He was busy with business, but he had to visit the sacred water fountain for once to see, if there is healing possible for a friend.

The king bowed before the water source and asks kindly, please can you give us release from this sickness, my friend he is very weak and surely doesn't want to die, but he wants to live.
With a tender gesture the king unfolds his hands and the water fountain embraces him with a dear sound.

Please take a cup and bring it to the friend, he shall drink from me. Half with his eyes closed and then bring him to my friend, the warm spring in the mountains. There he can find relieve and be at peace and serenity. He shall find his relieve within a short period of time.

Even the king did not know about this termal source in the mountains, but he surely wants to find out and bring his friend to out. Hot springs are natural appearances of bringing hot water from the earth into a bath.
The king went back to his friend and wonders already happened. He was suddenly relieved. The king was so in fascination that he asks how can this be, we did not even go to the spring in the mountains. How can this be?
Spring in the mountains? Yes, there is a hot thermal spring in the mountains near by. Let's go and see.

The two friends now intrigued by the wonder of the source, really want to find out, what is behind the mysterious water source. Life is like a springing Source of happiness and livelihood, of many possibilities, so abundant and free.

So the two, the king and his friend, on the way to the thermal springs and there they met two pilgrims. I wonder where you are going, you must be the king, what a surprise! There are many ancient temples in these mountains and in the land there are many mysterious creatures, like speaking trees, or unicorns, so what are you looking for exactly?

The king, in a friendly says: We are following the Water and only the water, because it is the most holy of all the elements.
Just imagine, our whole body is water and in tune with the elements. Know that everything in life is connected to the water into the light. So let's Pilger together to that water source.
On the way the four pilgrims and counter an old lady. She seems to be looking for herbs or any other kind of flowers in the forest. Maybe she knows where the fountain is.

Oh yes, the fountain is very close, one can almost hear it from here. Listen in and one can hear the fountain from a far.
Be calm and listen. The soothing sound of a fountain appears and also one can notice a river that is just near by.

The soothing sound of water, the endless river streams.
All comes from a source that we keep in our dreams.
The mystical forest, the fountain of life, they all spring
With happiness and joy into life one can sing.

With the help of the water, everyone can be healed, with the help of the water, one can refresh and rejuvenate,. As we let it flow in the search to grow, there might be the sound we hear, there might be the crown of no fear, so we know, we are on water. We are all water.

Let's embrace the sounds and no fear of the grounds we are safe where we are the soothing elements always in balance always in harmony. The king and his friend and the pilgrims were now so close to the water source that they could not even understand their own words yet's it was clear that the thermal bath is just here. The king-size of leave finally we have found the mysterious source of the hot Springs. The spring seem to be healing I can feel it already. Now let's find a way to get into the bath. The pilgrims please stop for a devotional chant

Oh healing water, the source of life.

It also is warm what a surprise come, long and enjoy the endless stream can you hear the flow and the singing of the birds who are so happy that we are here now let's relax and have no fear. Now relax the whole body and imagine you are sitting in this wonderful hot spring constantly going into the bath we are sitting in and leaving into the nature becoming a river stream. There he sits and we find ourselves to be at ease. All healing want to please please please, take all our dirt. So cleansing and pure. We breathe in and out again. Equally in an equally out again. The king is happy and now says this spring of hot water shall be protected for the ever lasting stream of people coming here for healing and rejuvenation. Let's make this a natural paradise for everyone to see and you pilgrims you shall be the guards of this place as you love the water more than anyone. The pilgrims so delighted and happy know their duty is set.

As all the participants of the party listen to what the source says, suddenly it starts to speak: watch I am not the only one. There are more like me coming out of the ground making this precious sound up in the very hills deep in the caves there are more springing sources hidden. Like the fountain of the marketplace and the hot fountain here in the mountain there are many more of these precious springs. Some of them are yet to be explored and who has time and the courage to go can find them.

Now let's sit and meditate here at the source and feel how the water is cleansing you from within and from without.

Breathe and feel the pure rejuvenation that comes from the source, slowly and gently the water treats us well.

Be aware of the sound of the water and an endless rhythm sounding the vibration of life and making us happy just like that - it is joy, it is harmony, it is peace. Relax and find the ease within this piece. The water is also a body for the most part so we give thanks to the water.

We can also harmonize our system which is mostly water.
So within and without the water can help us for a good rest. As we appreciate the water we can harmonize and bring everything into balance. Water is balance. Let's embrace this harmony and balance of the water, wherever it may be. To be sure we can say water is with us but it doesn't belong to anyone it is free, always flowing. Always in the flow like the breath. So these elements, Water and air are like friends that like to explore and be together.

Together the air and the water are in union.
Now relax your whole body and the water in the soil and all the elements it is now time to rest and to bring full relaxation from the hand to the head to the chest to the belly to the feet. All of the parts of the body are now relaxed and in harmony like the water like the air that is constantly coming into the nostrils and going out of the nostrils.
Just equally breathe and let yourself return to the kingdom within.

The kingdom of your body is now safe and relaxed, fully conscious of all you are doing. Every sensation is equally part of your being and you find comfort and the little space of your heart. Where an endless fountain of good dreams is springing into the night.
As all are returning, we gently close our eyes and find the ease of the breeze. In and out, equally, coming and going. Just gentle and soft, the night shall be the river in which the fountain of joy and happiness springs.

Let's pray for all the beings, for all the water and for the every single drop of happiness in this universe.

May All be happy and well, may we all have a good night and sleep alright.

Creativity Story

<u>1483 words, 20 minutes</u>

To be creative means to truthfully use the energies that make creation. Now let's create a beautiful garden where we just sit in and meditate for the rest of our whole life. For the rest of our lives and for the life beyond we can create a life and life beyond. Everyone is the creator of their lives possibility, balance and harmony and eventually of their unity.

This might be a creative garden of unity so let's take our creative tools which are our imagination, it is like dreaming, and let's imagine ourselves on the wonderful green fields. One is sitting there with their eyes half open and half closed. We are there just breathing and doing nothing else. No worries about nothing, everything is in care, we are breathing we are alive, everything is there. Even though our friends are here with us and they can help with creating a beautiful garden of unity - let's imagine togetherness.

There may be a fountain in the middle of the garden which springs and brings creative water, so pure and fine, we are able to witness the water fountain also to create a ripple, into a stream, a small, beautiful river stream and we sit in this garden just breathing.

We witness and we become the playful creator of our garden of unity.
So what can bring us more into balance and peace? May it be our friends and family, let's bring them all here and see they are happy as we are happy, too. So we are sitting in this garden of unity and we are breathing and we are happy.

 Let there also be nice flowers because everyone likes to smell nice flowers, and you can imagine many flowers in many colours, in red and in orange, and yellow, in blue and in rose and in purple.
There is also a nice and wonderful rainbow hovering from one side with the sun over to the other side with the fountain creating a nice and lush rainbow in this garden of unity.

So there might be a happy family and friends and some nice animals. Whichever animals you like. This is the power of creativity, to imagine, everything is a possibility and everything is possible. Now you can be creative on your own. Just do as you like and form, shape, create the world as you like it to be. And you can see creativity which is with you and for all.

Just give yourself the space and allow yourself to be creative. Then creativity can blossom like a flower and it can spring like a fountain into the world. In any colour, in any shape. Of course we want to use it for something good, that's why say unity, because it is always good, bringing people together, joining friends and family and all being in happiness and peace.

Let's all be happy and creative. In our mind and our hearts we can be creative with our hands and likewise be healthy. We can be healthy and creative with our whole body. We can be joyful then in a place of harmony with our full being. We can be the creator of the garden. Caring, Creating, how to know, is all in your head and in your dreams. Let's meditate and see the creative flow of life that is coming from the hearts and going again. But as coming from the belly creativity is surrounding the whole being. This is everywhere and everything.

It is the light, it is the water, it is the fire and it is the earth and the air. Creativity is everything. It is music, it is our way to express the voice. So we can express the voice and listen to our own music. For us to be content and with it to be creative, means to be content. The voice the music and what we do is creativity, so all you see and all you feel, or all you touch. This is one Creation, and where does this creation come from?

It is all within the self, within the body, mind and spirit, so lets explore the mysterious world of creativity.

We sit silent and equanimous in the Garden of Unity and feel at home, just like that. Breathing, equally in and equally out. Our place in this Garden is always there and we can always come back here as we wish. Just bring your awareness to the heart and here you are in the garden of unity. Now let's breathe and find a huge brush, a magic brush that allows us to brush with our eyes and paint in all the colours we like. We can brush with our eyes and paint it all. We may paint from the top of the head, to the right, to the bottom and to the left, we paint all around in circles and we can twinkle with our magic creative eye brush. Twinkle and paint, how you feel like.

The feelings are like to motor of our creativity. It is driving our creativity and bringing life to our creation. So when we feel grounded and close to earth, our creation might appear in a brown or red. When we are happy and joyful, it might appear in an orange or light gold, as we are all creators one can co-create with a friend. It is easier to make rainbows as together one has more creative freedom.

The source of creativity comes from our belly, from the connection to our Mothers and the connection to our Mother Earth. One can nurture this connection by breathing into the belly, slowly and gently in and softly letting go. Put one hand on the belly and feel how the air is steaming into the body and belly lifting up, like a balloon. The belly is lifting up and the air circulates in the belly. Just focus on the breathing and the ups and downs of the belly. It is coming like waves, rising and passing, rising up inhale and passing away, exhale. Let this be rhythmic and equal. Equally in and out again. Gently in and out again. The breathing is balanced and equal, our mind is steady and peaceful. We celebrate every breath and feel the ups and downs. From the source, the connection to one's Mother energy can flourish and we imagine a beautiful bright orange flower blossoming. So bright and beautiful it blossoms into every direction, to the left and right, the below and high, the belly feels fine and the orange blossom opens every single petal for a wonderful light.

One can see this light flowering and opening further and further the light expands and a golden shimmering glow enlightens the whole body. All the body parts are now surrounded in golden light of creativity, with a smile we can acknowledge and find serenity.

We breathe and by breathing the golden smile and the light expands even further into the atmosphere where it spreads and comes to life. Creativity in person is now alive and we have the chance to greet and welcome the creativity we see, a person wearing a gold cloak, surrounded with beautiful shimmering light. This person is just here for us, bringing us peace and joy.

We shall walk in the garden of unity to find a nice place for the sunset, where the rainbow meets the horizon there is also the sun setting for a good night. Therefore we trust the creative world, our creative world and we follow along to seek out a nice and comfortable place for the sunset celebrations. The birds are tweeting, the bees are humming and all is in care, the creation is now in full swing, changing, like the seasons, like we change our garments, from golden to blue, to purple and into the night.

There might, there might be the light of the setting sun, creative as always, it creates a scene of splendor and serenity, the celebration of light to transform into the night.

That's right, let's celebrate this way with a smile and appreciation. Thank you dear sunshine, thank you Mother Earth, that I am here and alive. Thanks for everything, for all the friends, for the family, and for the garden of unity.

Thanks for the birds that sing and everything like the stars and the moon, like the heaven and the air we breathe. Breathe in and relax for a good night. The foremost last sun beams set the sky into colours and like a huge hand has created a wonderful picture, creation is always in flow, ever changing with the eternal glow. One might never forget to thank.

All my thanks to the world,
All the love into the world,
All the happiness and kindness,
All the Unity.

May All beings experience unity and happiness.
May all be free to do, to be, creative and alive.

Let it be a good, good night.
Rest and sleep well.

River Story

<u>1507 words, 20 minutes</u>

Once upon a time there was a river of milk. It was a precious river flowing through the land with the bees and the flowers living in harmony with the human kind. The land was so rich and abundant all the beings were happy and at peace. The river of milk was coming from the source up in the highest mountains. The source was well hidden and no one could reach the source, only by guidance of the priest. This guidance can only be attained when one is humbly serving the whole of the community. So once in a lifetime when a member of the community was giving birth the priest went up to the mountains to fetch a silver cup of milk from this source. This milk was considered holy in this land and it became the link to the divine. This connector called nectar was purified and so rich in minerals it could bring the newborn child to live more than 100 years. In this life time one just has to do the service and one also has to obey the principles of the community like no harming, so being peaceful, and no stealing, in general being of good attitude and peaceful character. One could also be initiated into the livelihood as a monk who'd so be able to drink from the source of all life.

One day it came rain from the heavens and all the people were wondering why is it white rain? It was a special day only every 500 years there is an occasion in the sky where the Milky Way beats with me the rhythm of the milky River like two heartbeats in synchronicity.

So now in this land there was a river of milk flowing and the rainfall bringing new life to the land where the river could not reach and everyone was celebrating the present of life, growing fruits and crops and all one needs for life so one could sustain and live happy and peaceful. When one grows older one can bathe in the river. It is possible that one can be in the river, we just have to imagine it and believe.

With the breathing we can bathe, we can breathe in the stream of peace and purity. This pure and peaceful stream can flow in and around us and protect us and also make us young to live a long life. The ancient Scriptures say that the pool holds the nectar of immortality. This nectar was once brewed on the occassion of creation, where the guides of the heavens came together to brew a milky soup of endless life. A great recipe needs great cooks.

So the best cooks in the whole universe came together to create the world with the help of one special ingredient. It is in the Milky Way and it is always growing from the river. It is a brilliant, most fragrant ingredient that one can find nearby, very close actually, in colours that are pure and translucent, sometimes it has a protection though and one has to be careful to obtain this precious ingredient.

So the Gods were collecting it and bringing it to the soup of Milk where all the heaven guides were watching the process happening and of course the steam was rising from the heat that was made by the eternal flame provided from the ever-lasting woods, from the mystical forests.

Brewing this sacred soup of milk it yet had to be churned, so there came the Mother of All beings with a golden spoon to churn the wonderful mixture into existence and therefore all the creation came into play. This is why the sun and earth are rotating, anyway, this is why this land has a river of milk, because in this process there had to be someone trying this mixture and the youngest one was first.

So one got a silver cup and filled it in. This filling was the first source of the Milky stream that momentarily still flows in the sacred land of immortality. This river of milk is also with us, we just have to breathe and one can feel that this river comes into existence with every breath. The wonderful story dates back to the reign of the first Gods and Godesses that create the Milky Way, in a long way, they made the animals, plants and all beings harmonize by giving all the beings some sort of nectar.

This nectar is still in flow, and through long and persistent service for the community attainable. One can taste this nectar and also dive into the vast milk ocean, where the river of milk ends in. This is a long way of constantly doing good for others an obeying the rules and regulations of the saintly ones, like Father and Mother.

Mother Earth is still churning this Giant Milk Soup and we are all a part of this process, breathing and living gives the texture and serving gives the taste. It is essential like breathing and one can be in happiness, like the people of the lands with the milk river flows.

From that land there is a warrior who earned his livelihood by achieving super feats like holding the breath for long times to dive with the underwater creatures or he got to very high mountains just to meet the angels living there. He renounced fighting long-time ago to celebrate life and learn how to be immortal, hence he came to the land of the Milky River. Wherever he walked people were curious, what does such a fierce warrior do here? He is not fighting but he is looking for something.

A small boy came up to him asking what is going on and why the search, and the warrior in full surrender bows to the young one to tell him, that he hears the sound of the river every night in his dreams and he just closed his eyes to follow the stream of sound, therefore he came here to the land of immortal milky river streams. The boy smiles and suggest him to go to the local priest, he is the father of the village governor and the chief of the river protection program. There is a milky river protection program house just down the road, find the Priest Avalan there.

Avalan is of great statue and a wise man with a calm gaze, please have a seat and lets prepare my favorite tea. The warrior did not come for tea, but he knew waiting in patience is good service. So he waits and the tea is ready, it is a welcome tea Avalon says, as one travels so far just to come here, we are heartily welcoming our guest with a warm tea and later you can have a warm milk. Everything here is making us live a long and healthy life, you know, the fresh air and the purity of the river, all give us a good day and night. This happens every day, and night, hence we seem to be living immortal.

There is a story of trader who wanted to sell all his gold for a glass of this milk and he came here with his whole family. When he arrived he was surprised, he did not even have to trade anything, he just received a nice glass of rejuvenating milk. Then he started to laugh and dance and sing. What a scene, he was so happy, immortal in that sense of joyful and at total ease. Happy and at peace.

Another time there came a beggar here and he was just thirsty, what a surprise it must be hard walking up these hills, isn't it?
The warrior nods and finds his cup already full again, please drink and have some more. There is plenty, it is an abundant source up there, but we are keeping it for the newborn who drink a cup of this milk and remain always young at heart. Young at heart, smiling, and kind. Compassionate with all beings and ever living in harmony.

Just breathe and relax, also for the night you can stay by the river and in the morning you might take a dip in this holy place. Totally happy the warrior sips and listens to the wise man talk, yet Avalan knows it's almost sunset and the night comes in, he better prepares and brings his children to bed, there is also a little

celebration with candle lights and butter lamps. These are especially beautiful at night. Watch the ceremony with me please, and join for a warm milky treat, into the Milky Way.
Now two strangers became friends and the warrior forever lived on in this land of immortality to help the priest lighting the candles and butter lamps. In a lifetime of good service and with Love and devotion one can be free, to live in peace, love and harmony.

Enjoy the endless stream of happiness and rest, sleep well and dream on.

Friendship Story

<u>1491 words, 20 minutes</u>

Friends are the essence of life. Let's embrace that and find ourselves in healthy and nurturing relationships as friends and maybe even as long life friends.

Relax your body and find yourself safe and secure in the space of love. Around you, you're being surrounded with a shimmer of light that glows and brings about peace and harmony. This light we breathe and we can feel.

The light of friendship is like the smile. You can see it as soon as you smile honestly, one smiles back. This light of your love, smiling, is the power of friendship. Let's embrace that and find ourselves calm, breathing, feeling and breathing's fully out again. The breathing is equal and the in-breath matches the out-breath. The breathing is natural and the constant flow is audible. You can hear the breathing coming in and going out.

Now you can close your eyes and find yourself in this space of imagination where you sit comfortable on green moss so mild like a cushion and so soft that you sink into this place and it may be a place of peace and harmony. So as you are. Breathing in and equally breathing out again. There's nothing to worry about, we are just trusting the love of nature and the friendship of our breath as our breath is our long life friend.

Smile and say hello to the breath. Embrace the breath. And let the breath go again. It's a constant coming and going. And whatever is happening around you, find yourself always be in balance with the breath as the rhythm goes.

The rhythm might be fast and one can notice if the life is fast right now in this moment, or the breath might be slow, maybe life might be of a slow moment right now. So whatever moment is happening is happening in the breath. The breath is our friend and one might know when to say hello as the friend is coming again and again. And one also knows to welcome the breath with joy and with a smile.

Oh hello you wonderful breath of life, you are my friend coming home. Then there is space for celebration, for love and for life. This is the life happening within you. When the life has happened we have to say goodbye again. This goodbye is a chance to make room and to let go, maybe this friend likes to go with the present.

Like here, bring the peace and take this love, and maybe here you have a smile for your way out. So we let go and the ever-lasting friends go away with love and peace and a smile. When your friend has left, there is enough space to embrace for another time your friend will come.

Breathe in and let your friend the life air come into the nostrils and let your friends go again leaving the nostrils. Every time we breathe we have the chance to equip our friend with a message, and whatever this message may be, one can come up with the one, message going into the world.

This is why we can speak in prayer for the world. This is why we can hope for friendship in the world. Hence we speak it out, and devotion and love. Let's pray.

May all beings be happy,
may all beings be at peace,
may all beings be friends,
like the best friends one can be.

To enhance the potency of this prayer we can speak it louder and we can speak it more often, so one can repeat that prayer again and again.
May all beings be happy
May all beings be at peace
May all beings be friends.
So we are still sitting on the most in a beautiful friendship garden and in this garden there is much friendliness, even the birds, the bees and the trees. And so we could just sit here when all of the beings come to us, and we can greet them with a smile.

The beings smile back in this world's unity, in this garden the friendship is present. Let's also think about our real life friends, let's imagine them and invite them kindly with a smile. All we see, them smiling back and there we go, let's be together in this Garden of friendship.

The sun is shining and the weather is nice, we are able to enjoy the sound of the birds and the song of nature. It is like a concert just for us, the music is so beautiful and harmonious we find our balance here.

See now and it's a blessing, we are here. Now, let's embrace that and feel the breath again. Notice the breath streaming in the nostrils and out again, and find the rhythm to be equal, and the heartbeat in synchronicity.

This synchronicity feels so good to us, it is like a shelter, coming home, to the garden of friendship. We can walk around now and search for something that is interesting for us. Maybe we find the tree with special leaves, or maybe we find a flower with this specific cense, but we do really, is just observing.

We see ourselves playing, we see ourselves wondering in the forest full of adventure, we are witnessing the constant stream of life, like rivers and water flow and our friends they like to be with us.

So together we are exploring this friendship garden, so together we are exploring our friendship, so together we are living in harmony. There is no fight, there's just the pulse of life, that makes us live and feel encouraged, and it makes us smile and happy to be who we want to be.

Let's embrace that and let's embrace the breath, let's embrace our friends and the place we are playing in. This place is in our heart so let's embrace the heart. From this place, it also is in our minds so let's embrace the mind and the imagination. Let's embrace our friends and family and let's embrace the whole world as friends and family.

Now see yourself in this friendship garden and from your heart there is a silver light shining into the hands and the hands embrace each other, bringing the palms together, and now the light shines from the middle of your head into the wide wide world.

May all beings be friends, playing in the friendship garden. May all beings be happy, may all be at peace.

So let's find the breath again and the breathing goes in and out, with saying hello to the breath and with a goodbye we are letting the breathing go. Everything is in harmony and now in this friendship garden we have time to celebrate, so let's bring everyone together and celebrate this friendship.

The birds are bringing their favorite songs, the elephants are bringing their favorite foods, the monkeys are bringing their favorite bananas, the ducks are bringing their favorite dress. The trees that bring their favorite flowers and the flowers bring their favorite cense. The bees are bringing their favorite honey and all the friends are coming together.

There is a wonderful celebration for the sunset, waiting for the night as the sun brought his favorite friends the moon. And the moon brought her favorite friends the stars, and the stars brought their favorite friends the Stardust. In this Stardust is a wonderful dream to the nice night as it is coming just while the sun sets.

All the animals, all the people, all the flowers and the insects as well as the sun and the moon are now watching and we are here to all speak a prayer together:
May all beings be happy
May all beings be free
May all live in harmony in this friendship garden.

We are gently closing the night as everyone gently says goodbye with a smile, we also smile and put our palms together again to give thanks. We close our eyes and be content with this wonderful friendship garden where we can return every time even in the night.

Now relax your whole body and feel the life of your breath slowly and gently calming and becoming smooth. Now find yourself in peace and harmony with all the beings around.
May it be a good night. May the stars shine bright, it's the moon singing a song for peace and harmony. Rest relax and sleep well.

Everything in life is free,
the friendship, the breathing,
the peace and harmony.
We come to this life
With the help of the light.
From the stars and sun,
Life can sprout and begun.

Everything in life is free,
The stars and the sun,
The peace and harmony,
To hold it dear kind,
Is just a state of mind,
To bring it forth and go,
We are the one to know.

Everything in life is free,
The peace, love and harmony.

Mermaid story

<u>1508 words, 20 minutes</u>

Once upon a time there was a Harbor city and three young salesmen that were doing their sales on the sea. Sailing from one continent to another to collect the most precious stories. Together they were sitting at the harbour and wondering where the journey will be going.

One of them was Chris, and Chris loves the orient so he wanted to go to the desert lands, anywhere close to the pyramids and the forgotten Harbour cities of the ancient empires. The other one, Momo, he wanted to go to the faraway lands of India and the Pacific ocean, where there are many stories to be told. The third one, J, wanted to go to the south, where there are many paradise islands with nice people and endless coconuts.

With this journey and to decide where to go, they needed help, so they asked the mermaid for help. She was living in an underwater cave just close to the harbour. And every time she sang a beautiful song, where she was praising the wonderful world's of this Neptune's Union.

This place is hidden under the water and is just reachable by the guidance of the water friends. So one of the three adventurous explorers right away starting begging the mermaid asking how can we reach this place. Neptune's union holds many mysteries and stories and the three were very engaged in finding this place.

The mermaid said: Make sure you have the right attitudes of collecting stories and only collecting stories. Then I will make the preparations for your adventure. So the three promise, clearly understanding the preparations for the adventure and only stories might be collected.

With this preparation the three also had to prepare for the underwater, so they were crafting an undersea bubble. It is the bubble of light with an infinite breath. It is the bubble around the head and it can support long long times underwater. It is an imaginary bubble of breath, but it works just like the normal one.

So there are three adventurous young friends collecting stories for now and later, on their way to explore the mermaid's advice, to go to Neptune's union. With the help of the mermaid the three are diving deep into the blue blue ocean and deeper and deeper until the mermaid says, here that's the entrance.

The entrance is beautifully decorated and two mermen with a bright gaze looked at the three adventurous seafarer. The mermaid explains, these three are here to hear the best stories of Neptune's union so please let them in. They will remain only in peace and serenity as these three will do no harm.

Please show them the wonderful world of this mighty place. The mermen are astonished and open the entrance for the three adventures. The mermaid says now you are on your own.

The first story they hear is via a simple underwater worker. He is busy collecting shells for the underwater celebrations as these shells serve as instruments, as musical instruments. Even the high priests blow these shells for big ceremonies, and the worker tells them how he has to be careful to select only the prettiest and best shells. But eventually when the work is finished he goes back to his family to find everyone safe at home.
 When everyone is welcome, they go for the market. The three companions are very happy to hear the story, because they love markets. Now they're heading onto the market to hear more stories. You are well invited to join for the market since the working is over I can get you there.

At the markets the mermaids and mermen are in full swing bringing goods like underwater spices, plankton, shells and all other gifts from the underwater world to the people. The sharing is caring, he says and we talk to a local underwater salesman who was very delighted to see salesmen from the overwater world.

The world's maybe different but the trading is the same, it is like a constant coming and going like the waves of the shore of the ocean. With a breeze maybe the tides they come and go. Like the breathing coming and going.

We are happy to hear and now proceed to the middle of the market where there is this stage and we listen to an underwater artist chanting a beautiful underwater song.
Under the sea, all be happy, all be free, to eternity, happy and free, and we and the winds, and the union of all the water around Neptune.

Next we are visiting a school of the Neptune Union, in midst the underwater caves, says the mermaid merchant: He bows and tells a story of how he established a school here in the underwater world. I saw many schools in my times on the shores of the earth and I knew education and a safe learning environment is important, so I funded this school with the help of the Union.

It is a blessing that even Neptune himself came to the school to see the children play and learn. This is the way, let's walk it together and one can see a beautiful building carved into the underwater caves and there, very well protected, play the children around in an underwater schoolyard.

The school is visited by sea turtles, little children fish, tiny sharks and whales as well as mermaids and mermen that serve here as teachers. Education and sea knowledge is important, because did you know that more than 70 percent of this body and equally of the earth is a body of water?

Water is the element of balance and serenity. With the help of the land it is holding the balance of all beings. Some sciences believe that the first creature ever living on earth came from the ocean. The vast ocean and the sea are salty, where as the lakes and springs are sweet. What would you say is the taste of water?
Maybe have a cup of water, because water is necessary in our everyday life.

Everyone shall love and appreciate the water, as we do. Here we learn to embrace the water and to keep It clean. We are also collecting findings in the sea, like wracks or treasures. Other things we are upcycling again, so it can be used for ones benefit. Some of the school materials are recycled, we can do a lot and help to keep the planet beautiful.

We also like beautiful things that's why we play music, make art or dance. Everyday there is a sunset festival, where we celebrate the world of the water and the light.

This is a spectacle and you are free to join us into the night. Merman and mermaids like to party and then head home to have good night stories read by the wise fathers and mothers. These are the best way to have a soothing and calm night.

Sometimes Neptune comes by to witness the festivals and there are many stories around his personality. One knows he is of fair blue skin with a big crown on his head, he likes to enjoy the arts and music, even one time he left his throne to dance with the little ones and gave his favorite speech after.

We all have to be wise and conscious of the breath, he said, we have to be wise and conscious of the behavior and therefore let's embrace that, first with the breath. It is the air that connects us all, living beings and it is the water and the light, lets come to unity with all the beings under and over waters, let's make the first step and invite people into our Union.

This is why we are, also, to craft a relationship of friendship from under the sea to the earth and sky alike. All beings shall live in harmony and peace. Let's play and sing together into the sunset. The night is coming.

We are all beings here on earth, living for service and kindness, bringing the world together, thank you, that you are here. It is a blessing and a wish, to bring all the world to unity.

The dance and songs are going into the night and we are breathing through, as the three explorers are on their way upwards to the surface, what they have heard is worth more than just one story, and everyone had their favorite part of the under water world, what was yours?

Let's get back to land and give thanks to the mermaid that gave us entry into this wide world of discovery and let's thank Neptune's Union to bring a new perspective into the night, maybe we dream on and there we prepare and relax the whole body. From the head to the tippy toes, we relax the whole being and find ourselves in serenity and peace. All is in Union, as we come to Balance and Harmony:
A good night this one shall be. Rest, relax and sleep well.

Sea Travel Story

<u>1487 words, 20 minutes</u>

In times of Travel one can discover the Self.

Once upon a time there were three friends, Chris, Momo and Jo, who all loved the sea as they lived most of their lives in a Harbour city. Trading was their great gift and finding good stories their duty. They all wanted to go around the world but only now it is possible, as they have left home to set sail for an adventure around the world. First the three friends had come over the home sickness, therefore they collected their favorite stories of their families and friends to carry them always home while on the sea.

The sea is full of fish but there also other beings like mermaids and underwater cities. There are also hidden treasures and interesting findings like new species. One has to be careful, and very attentive with the sea and the waters, as the waters are precious and sensible. After all the sailing the three friends believe to protect the sea as much of a part as travel by sea with the wind and with the weather, we are all depending.

Dependent of the water because essentially we are water. The three step on board over the plank onto a wooden sailboat with five masts. The boat is named Hernanda, and has sailed the seven seas many times. The seven seas are also now in sight for the three adventurers. As long as we are finding what we are looking for, says Momo, as long as we are remaining friends says Chris and as long as I can breathe fresh air says Jo. All is fine and the ship takes off to the endless shores of discovery.
The wind is blowing, the waves are mild and peaceful and the three are looking forward for their first destination.

The shores of a never ending Discovery offer fresh air to breathe and more. The discovery brings the explorers closer to themselves. Let's breathe through with the seafarers and hope for good winds. As the wind allows one to be able to move, one sets sail with the help of the life air, we breathe - we live.

Breathe and come along a journey where we explore the beauty of the breath. Can you hear it? It is with us. Inhale, Exhale. Can you hear the wind coming in and going out again? Can you feel the intensity of the air? The fresh, cool air, it allows us to live and explore. We can be in harmony with all. All is breathing and alive. Let's embrace that and follow the flow.

The friends are now in the middle of the vast sea and there we spot the first great discovery. It must be an animal as large as the vessel, it splashed a fin and a high fountain of water rises into the air, as it seems to be breathing, we might find a friend in this being. This being has a long tail, like a giant fish and it has black skin and a white belly, as well as a large mouth. Luckily it seems to play and have fun. The fin splashes again into the water and a large water tower elevates into the air.

The water is the great connection.
I am water, you are water, we are all connected with the water. The water is us. One is with the soothing balance, the harmony and unity, as we are all on the same sea. Let's sea and find how the water giant is doing. Chris calls out: Hey, big friend, are you okay? We can help you we are here on the sea. Let's unite together in harmony, as we are all part of the water. Let's find a way.

I am the protector of the Underwater City, and My name is Elias the White Humpback Whale. I am the benefactor or all under water creatures and I am glad to meet you, because I heard you like to save and protect the precious stories of the water world.
This is your chance to have a meeting with my friends just follow me.

We can believe this wonderful incident, this beautiful and giant creature just invited us for a water party, well, the three sailors are more than happy, and yes we are here to protect and connect for experience. As we gain experience we can live a life of peace and trust.
Let's breathe in deeply, and follow Elias tor a new discovery.

Just see, we whales are only feeding of what's already in the sea, oh there is Lizy and there is Josiah, my brother and sister, we are vegetarians and have always been. As we are famous for our songs, we like to introduce you to hump back whale singing.

The three giant whales open their mouths and a sonar of water sounds comes clear to our ears, unique in nature, the three add melodies and harmonies to their choir which soothes even the toughest seafarer.

Follow the whales,
Into the waves,
Hear their song
And forget all along,

All craving and desire,
The will to aspire,
Crystal clear sapphire,
Beautiful like water and fire.
Let's hear the rhythm of the sea,
See, one can feel the harmony.
Let the whales show you how to be,
In Peace, Love and Unity.

The endless waves of bliss touch the hearts of the three seafarers and the endless curiosity became still for a moment. The moment of the whale song remains back on board. What a masterpiece! With a big gasp of fresh air the three come back to their journey, but how can one be so Gigantic just by eating greens?

Anyway the wind never stops
And blows the three towards the wide sea where now Dolphins play around the vessel shaking their heads in an asking manner, what is it that you are looking for, come we have a treasure, right below, the three just wink and say: Hey, we are safe here on board, but you are smart enough to know, that we have all the treasures with us and our stories.
The Dolphins laugh and one starts to sing a Dolphin song.

Three seafarers look for new hope and land, otherwise we could not give you a hand, because we only have fins, and a blow hole, see the water coming out of the whole!

The dolphins blow a nice water fountain out of their blow hole and the three sailors get a large dolphin shower, but they start to laugh and that's normal on the sea, you might get wet by a dolphin who likes to play.

Even further down the sea the three come to make the next discovery, close to an island, not so far away, there is a wise turtle with a soothing grin and a whole family on its back.
All the turtles seem to be so content and kind around this wise and old turtle. There is an aura of peace surrounding this family and the three explorers become very warm-hearted.
This is what we are looking for, away from home we have collected all these stories, but what is the first chapter of ones life? It is the raise from a baby to a child, the wonderful journey from the first steps to the first words, the first school visit and the first date.

All we are doing now is leaving it behind, even though we can be in between.
Let's breathe once more this wonderful fresh air of the wide and free world of liberty and remain with this sight of the peaceful turtle and its family.
The turtle smiles and the three are on a way home for good, knowing their mothers and fathers, brothers and sisters, Uncles and aunts, as well as all the friends are waiting. Now they have beautiful stories of the whales, the giant protectors of the sea, the dolphins that love to play and blow water from a hole and the most lovely turtle, so old and wise, taking care of all the family.

In serenity all the ocean and sea needs to be safe and protected, all three agree, it is a previous gem of lives that come to live like us, in peace and with family. All the lives matter in this vast world, as the three come home, all have gathered to hear a bit of their journeys, yet the travelers are just happy to be embraced and to have the same old feeling of home again.
Coming home is like coming to rest, to ones own body, which we fully know and trust. Know the breath and one shall know the waves, and tides, of the endless ocean of discovery. Life is a wonderful journey, as we breathe, as we relax into the good good night.
Dream on the vast ocean of possibility, rest, relax and sleep well.

Whale Story

1483 words, 20 minutes

This is the story of Elias the Whale, a white humpback whale who grows up in the vast ocean near the shores of a continent we know as Australia. Elias knows all the ocean around this island continent and is content to be with his family. His sister Lizzie and his brother Josiah are equally a humpback whale living as a happy family In the ocean. All of them are vegetarian, as they only eat the green plankton which they find in the sea. As Elias is now together with his family they swim to another vacation destination.

They want to make holiday on the beautiful shores of the Gold Coast. This is where people are very friendly out to the white whales: Elias loves the people and when he sees one on the boat or on the shore he splashes with his fin a huge water tower into the air. So one can see that there is a whale. Wow look at this whale! Elias and his family are also well known for that song, as whales are beautiful singers. It is like a long tone from the mouth of the whale that vibrates for hundreds of Kilometers in the ocean and other whales can hear it even very far away. This is how whales communicate.

A whale sound goes like that, AWUHUWAAA.
He is a fish in the sea, a very large and precious one. One day Elias will become the father of a family who is the single singer of the orchestra. Hearing this song one might know that he is Elias the whale with a beautiful show. Everyone is unique, with the unique voice to show. Elias is the one to make the people happy.

Now let's breathe deeply and imagine we are on the vast ocean of the sea, to see that there is a splash in the distance, this must be Elias! On the Gold Coast with the chance to come close to Elias and his family, the whale gives us a show blowing a huge water fountain from his blow hole, singing and playing.

One can be mesmerized by this sight, as the sun shines bright the whales are also very wise, growing up to 15 metres long just by eating greens. This is how important it is to stay healthy and fit. Elias also moves a lot swimming many kilometres in the ocean every day, isn't that fascinating? Let's dive and swim with the Whale.

Imagine there's a protective bubble around you. We are breathing in this protective bubble, it is our protection to go under the sea. We are noticing the breath, how the breath is coming into the nostrils and going out again. The breath is always the central life force, so always keep track. Let's embrace the protection and come back to the underwater world where Elias lives.

Come along to our home, Elias is very excited that we are here with him and hopes he can make a good impression so we know how whales live under the sea. Essentially they don't have a TV or Sofa, they rest while gliding on a wave, just closing their eyes for a moment and knowing everything will be fine. The water shall carry one away. Into the nice and soothing dreams of a whale we find ourselves in midst the beautiful underwater world, where the water is crystal clear and wild. The waves are sometimes bigger than buildings but now the waves are calm and tranquil. Watch the waves of the ocean coming and going out again. The beautiful synchronicity of the wind and of the waves is the matter that moves the world.

Elias knows everything about the waves, but he knows only so little about the winds. However Elias knows the breath, even under water he can breathe and find balance in the breathing. He is fully aware of the movement, because the water is never still, here in the ocean there is always movement and dynamism. The wonderful thing is, Elias also loves to travel, together with his family he can use the movement to travel wherever he likes.

The family around Elias loves to travel too so they travel from the Gold Coast to the beautiful Shores of the Silver Coast. Here there are many fish living and there is also the families teacher living. He showed the family all about the surrounding of people and how to interact with humans. Elias was one of his best students. The sea is also full of interesting caves and ship wracks where sometimes divers come, to explore the wide variety in colourful fish. Yes, the ocean really is a stunning place for discovery:

So many whales that live here happily and free,
Wild it is but there is serenity.
All whales come along very well,
There is no harm as all are well and wise
What a surprise the sound of a whale,
Soothing and bright in nature
Announces a happy birthday,
Elias the underwater giant,

Knowing the people so well,
Is now celebrated with a special shell.
It makes a sound that is nice and loud,
Elias happily splashes and brings the water out,
From his blow hole the water shoots into the air.
Happy and joyful whales celebrate together,
Always moving with the water flow,
Gladly we are the ones to know,
How the whales come together in peace and unity.
May All beings live together in serenity.
Like the ocean all beings shall be protected,
And kept pure and clean, like the water crystal clear.
We are here, breathing underwater in a protective bubble just exploring and finding a new way, in midst the underwater trees and plants, shining in beautiful colours we glance. Thanks to Elias showing us the wide world of the ocean, bringing us closer to the shore, Elias helps us and we can hop on the whales back, which has a bump , that's why humpback whale.

Riding on the whales back we travel through the sea, knowing the protecting and security we hold on very well, so we keep the balance of the travel way. Where would one like to go on a back of the whale? Maybe to a safe haven or shore, maybe into the night, we are finding a nice sunset spot, alright.

From the waters the glitter of the sun, intense and bright, shimmers on the surface of the incoming night: The colours shift, the night comes in, in peace we cheer the sight, a golden ball sets into the sea, we find there is a tomorrow and there might be eternity. As the waves are coming and going, rising and passing away, everything is here to sway, up and down, from left to right and back, into the night. Let's celebrate the sight and one might find that everything is alright. The whales are sounding their favourite tunes.

Thank you world for the light, and for the night,
We love the ocean, we love the sea,
Everything is a small part of thee, whole, harmony.

Together we find family and the peace and serenity.
Like the waves come to shore, we come to ease,
Let's find serenity and peace.
May All beings under and over water be safe and sound,
May all beings be happy even to the deepest ground,

May all beings be helped and found,
Safe, and serene and sound.

All is good and we gently see the first stars in the sky, the moon appears likewise; too.
By the energy of the sun and moon, the tides come and go, by the power of the breath our life comes and goes. Let's breathe in peace and serenity and let's go for a good night.

We breathe into a good night and we let go for a goodbye. Breathing in and out. Thanks and all the appreciation for Elias and the whale family, as well as to all the whale family. All appreciation to the protectors of the sea, let's keep it pure and clean. The power of the ocean is with its inhabitants, as the ocean is just a part of earth, we are all here to keep and maintain the peace and serenity.

Elias also gives thanks with a beautiful whale sound: AWUHUWAAA and splashes once more giant masses of good night water into the star-sprinkled air. The light of the moon cools the senses and Elias dives back into the deep traveling ocean to maybe one day come close to you again, but until we can dream to swim with the whales and we can keep the connection with our breath, as all the beings are connected with the breath, with the water, the light.

Let's all be happy and content in this peaceful night,
Let's all share the way to be alright,
Let's all embrace the light,
Even in the good good night,
Sleep well and rest alright.

Dolphin story

1503 words, 20 minutes

Once upon a time there lived playful dolphins in the wide, wide ocean. They were so playful, they were even considered playful dolphins, but no zoo nor any man could ever keep them, they were so playful, they remained In wild freedom.

The freedom of the dolphin, is to be active and to roam around on the waves and in the ocean. As a dolphin plays it sometimes forgets the time and space and it can even become night and the dolphin would not know. Yet the dolphins are very intelligent and they know all the games of the underwater animals. Sometimes even Sharks, they were so smart, that they were outplayed by the dolphins as the Dolphins are just so clever communicating that no single animal has a chance.

It is the radiant sound of a dolphin that makes it noticeably beautiful, sometimes so beautiful other sea animals like sharks just fall in love with the dolphins, as the dolphins all look alike, they bring another dolphin to play and hence one can not decide which one is the more beautiful. This works every time. Also dolphins are very attentive to playmates and friends, they celebrate every day as friends day and therefore show their affection by singing or even touching nose to nose.

This is a sign of a lovely devotion towards one another. The affection is also expressed by laughing and smiling, because after a long day of swimming and playing, the dolphins are very tired, however they can relax best while laughing and singing soothing songs.

Under the sea, we are happy, laughing and cheering the Day,
We are always happy, as we have friends and family.

The sea is our home and we play our favourite songs each and every day, we feel alright and okay by the vast ocean grace, we also sometimes see a human face and when we do we laugh so much, that water springs from our blow hole and shoots out into the air.
Ha ha ha Ho Ho Ho Hu hu hu Hey hey hey hi hi hi.
Our love is all in care in the vast waters to sing and dance, yes we laugh and dance a lot and therefore praise the life. It is beautiful to be alive!

The dolphins jump out of the water to splash with a belly flap, and water rises into the air, sometimes so gracefully, we see the over water world. We like to jump and grow as friends, over the water we know there are no ends to the sky, the humans and beings alike, but we are dolphins the graceful beauty of the sea, swimming, singing and laughing in harmony. That might be, our destiny.

We come to explore the wide worlds of the blessed sea life, which never retires or stands still, always moving with the.wind, the waves come and go, and as well as one asks the dolphins to teach, how to be so gracefully in harmony with the sea.

Please dear dolphins, so magical and wild, how come you have the world of the waters so beautifully discovered and within? How do live so well with that?

You mean the fin? This like the legs you have and one can walk, but I am born deep in the sea and therefore we are here, and meant to be, a fin that moves up and down, left and right, is to navigate and feel, alright?

We are naval animals and long to be forever content with the waters, but you, it's all about being happy and at peace. Wherever we find ease. Our parents were the heirs of the sea and therefore we live here since we can see. So we just follow our parents and way to be happy. We also can breathe and therefore we are beings like you, living on this earth together with the water and the sun, with the light and the night.

We are dancing till the night, having to feel alive.
You are well invited to come with us, to see us dance and joyfully sing our playful chants.
Tonight there is a dolphin wedding and we celebrate the relationship of our dearest friend and singer, Sachran; the ever-funny and beautiful dolphin will be uniting with the dearest Sachruy who loves to be a dancing dolphin. One day they will show everyone how beautiful life of the underwater sea is. Hence they are practicing the art of underwater dance for their whole lives. They are inspired by their brothers and sisters who are all coming together to celebrate this wedding.

So come along to see the dolphin wedding harmony. The harmony starts with the big choir of many fishes and whales, as well as merman and mermaids who are likely to play the harps, under water shells and other musical sea instruments. There are underwater balloons and many visitors come from across the sea. Do you know this is the place of the wedding. Yeah, this wedding takes place! Let's dive in.

All the animals join together, to witness two dolphins unite and playfully have a reason to celebrate. Dolphins love to celebrate but even on a big wedding there is much going on, there are dolphins bringing underwater cakes, there are dolphins making underwater arts and craft for the kids, there is an underwater light show, and of coarse the choir is playing underwater music for everyone. As the bride is ready, cool drinks are handed to everyone, and the husband is speaking a toast to all the dolphin family.

I am glad, that we all can come here in peace and harmony, celebrating this unity. It is my wish and my blessing, that the whole ocean family comes together as one, to protect and playfully safe the ocean. The ocean is our greatest gift and we are so happy to have it. The ocean is like a big mother to us, and the earth is like the father that holds the ocean. We are all children of this world, and the only reason we are here, is because of our parents. So let's thank our parents. Let's all have a good time, and embrace the waters, playfully dancing, chanting, and being in harmony.

One can see, with the dolphins we have a good example of animals and a part of our earth. We all just want to live in harmony, yet we are acting differently, let's be aware of what we do and how one celebrates.

The dolphin party goes deep into the night, and everybody is sharing the site, happily uniting husband and bride swimming next to each other, in full sight. The party comes in full swing and beautifully the loved-ones are now to close the night with a last dance.

The last dance of the dolphins, only for this night, because they're dancing lights, will even shine into more nights. As the Waves come and go home, the shore remains the same, so the dolphin will ever be the best at this game in the sea, so come on, play fully, enjoying the waters in the sea, so beautifully, having always a reason to celebrate for life and for eternity.

Let's find out, how are the Dolphins are enjoying a good rest. As said, the dolphins like to laugh to relax, so let's try this. Ha ha ha, ho ho ho, hey hey hey, let the belly bounce. Just try your best to laugh like a dolphin, Ha ha ha, ho ho ho, hey hey hey, just feel the belly and laugh as loud as you can, don't worry about the neighbours, as laughing is the best remedy for relief, it is also good night medicine.

Just imagine the dolphins all together swimming into the night, under the nice moonlight, see them dancing and smiling, and just smile yourself. Be kind, and happy, with yourself, your parents and all around you. Remember the toast of the dolphin saying we are all one, every single one is a part of this earth? So how we live is key, and one might be as happy, joyfully and in harmony like the dolphins. Under the same moon, under the same light, may this be a blessed night.
Surround yourself with a crystal clear light and hear the sounds of the ocean, maybe one even hears the laughing of the dolphins, singing us a joyful song, relax and find ease with every single breath. Deeper and deeper we sink into the world of dreams where we are happily joined in protection and safe sound, by the voice and the ambient of the night.

There always is a light, even in the darkest night, one might be this, oh so bright, shining into the night, with a simple smile we can enlighten, even the darkest sea, with a smile, one might be able to see, what is peace, what is love, what is harmony.
Rest and relax for a good night.

Underwater Story

<u>1479 words, 20 minutes</u>

Once upon a time there was an underwater kingdom with a king and a queen. The kingdom was build next to an ocean, when a phenomenal earthquake happened and the city sunk into the depths of the ocean, this city is now inhabited by queen Zoronia and king Yuddha which are both native to the water. Like every good kingdom the queen and king loved to have celebrations, this time due to the birth of their first daughter which presented the kingdoms heritage. Down in the underwater city, the kingdom was part of an even larger kingdom under the guidance of Neptune, the King of the whole ocean.

When Neptune heard of the birth he was very delighted and sent his best guides to travel with him to the faraway underwater kingdom. The celebration shall takes place in the community square, where all the inhabitants of the small kingdom gathered. The dolphins brought themselves and some dolphin cake, the whales got their finest songs and the mermaids, as well as merman got themselves musical instruments to celebrate the new birth. Queen and King are happily joined by all the family members from the vast ocean family.

Underwater flowers are decorating the pathways and garlands of beautiful sea stars are given to the guests. Feel welcome and celebrate with us, it is a great day. There is also the King of the Ocean coming to celebrate with us. Many wonderful beings join around Neptune when he arrives and there he presents his birthday gift for the young one. It is a tiny conch shell for future music.

The priest are blowing this conch shell for procession and the whole ocean vibrates with joy and serenity. Even the turtles and little children turtles are there, even the oldest and wisest one.

The young and old, the wise and not so wise, the far and close ones all can celebrate together and the kingdom also knows to invite some people, like us, to their party as it is a beautiful spectacle they are sure, we like to see it, too.

Imagine crystal clear waters and an ancient underwater city that is alive and coloured in the most magnificent splendour, drenched in tastes and scents. All are welcome to join, and maybe we like to bring a friend to this celebration with us.

This is the chance to also think about a gift, what would we present, maybe a message, or maybe a happy birthday song.
Happy birthday to the princess of the underwater world. It's a beautiful appearance and the whole ocean is there to see the festivity.
The Queen and King are also happy, just sitting in the throne having a smile onto everyone. The birth of a newborn is always a delight and the baby is fully protected in a nice basket of gold and wool, safely slumbering.

We can imagine all the celebration just for one person, but the celebration is always on, as underwater creatures love to party and come together. Yet, we can imagine, it is probably the wide range and space in the ocean that makes it possible. Some kingdoms in the underwater world reach down to 10000, ten thousand metres, and these kingdoms are rarely visible, because in the depth there is pure darkness. Yet, there are still kings and queens living down there, and one of them is even coming to this celebration.

One may see, in the depth of the ocean, there is pure serenity, no stress, no tension, just watery peace, a gentle reminder of who we are - Peace.
The depth and darkness are one of a kind, yet this underwater kingdom shines with light. It is close to the shore in the Meditational sea, where bliss is essence and happiness to be.

We can dive into this sea and see it ourselves, the tranquility and peace are one of a kind. So prepare yourself with a breath and relax, because the more we relax, the deeper we dive. Into the ocean there are many mysteries unsolved, yet the place is safe and sound, with a guide, like Neptune, we can truly explore, breathing deeper and deeper, to the kingdoms door.

The entrance is clear and open for us to come, this is where the underwater journey has begun, a mermen is waiting for us to enter and we come in. It is a truly wonderful square, so vast and alive, well cared for and good, this is way to the Palast where the king and queen reside, just celebrating in full delight.

There is always reason to take it slow, with every breath we are the ones to know, breathing is light, even underwater we can, imagine, imagine, imagine.

Imagine all the fishes, living in this world,
Underwater, happy for today,
And tomorrow there shall be peace in every way.

Imagine all the colours, of the mermaids, dolphins and whales and there even is a fountain in the middle of the square bringing forth beautiful water bubbles of multicoloured goodness. Everything here seems so tender and soft, the waters are an element of balance. Even overcoming the biggest gap, water can reach everywhere without a miss. Even reaching the tops of the world, water disguised in snow can be every on this world.

In the air, under the Earth, in the Forest, and the sea,
Water is within and with us, to be.
We are waters as everyone is water, likewise connected with the elemental flow, springing from a source, growing up in water, rising to be born and living a life. The waters are ceaseless and always in flux, eternally adaptive and making us alive.

We can speak to the water and it listens to us, it is brave and tender at the same time. Water, is alive and always in flow, may give to understand, waters also know. Knowing the form and shapes of life, we can see that water is always here for balance and harmony.

In the Kingdom all are in Balance and harmony, within, waters make a way, we can be thankful for each and every day. Let's praise the water and give thanks for its delight, also when there comes a good night. Water adjusts and reflects what is there, light of the moon shimmers and the water is in care.
This is life, and life is water. Water is life and thankful we can be. Appreciate every drop and in abundance it may show, water springs, and comes in a flow. The waters are here to heal and nurture our growth, may one be fostered and held with life.

Thank you water, for making us feel alive, even in the good, good night.

We arrive at the kings throne to see the newborn and the queen are equally happy to see us. We are smiling in gratitude and hopefully we have a glimpse. Though we can see, a question arises in ourselves. What can I do to protect? Protect the water, as the water protects itself, protect yourself and the water is protected. The king smiles and adds, and maybe drink hot water in the morning, to start a good day, sometimes one can add some honey.
This recipe is by my grandma, the king gives us a wink and grins, let's celebrate the night under the moon light.

To say the least, the underwater life is magical, yet the parties are even more magnificent and we are helping us to a wonderful seat, where we can watch and witness the harmony, of the dolphins dancing with smily faces, the whales singing their ear-full songs, the merman are waving their flutes and harps, playing the melodies of joy and peace, and mermaids are bringing flowers to make everything look nice. What a surprise Neptune holds a speech:

May all water creatures live in harmony with thee, may all beings appreciate the waters we have and live in unity.

Let's celebrate this kingdom and welcome all our guests, that are coming here for a new quest. The quest is to protect and maintain, the precious, subtle and clear waters of the earth. By celebrating we hope to endure and praise the everlasting flow of life, that may rise and go, all the waters may rise and go, so does the night rise, and we shall have a good rest, so we are prepared to protect, with the help of the breath, we are here to live.

Let's live All in Peace, Love and Unity.

Let's also enjoy this scene and give our personal appreciation for what we have seen.

It has now been the chance to have a good night and further show our light, with a sincere smile we illuminate the night. May the stars twinkle, the moon beam and we find the peace, resting and relaxing, wholly, into the night.

Sleep well.

Rainbow story

<u>1635 words, 25 minutes</u>

Imagine a land of many possibilities, right away, but here for you to be. The place I am speaking of is in your imagination and here one can find endless worlds to discover. So, let's go for a walk and find a comfortable position to relax the body. Is the body relaxed, the mind and the imagination can blossom like a beautiful flower. This flower of the Self is within everyone's reach and can be attained by everyone. It is our human possibility, like a smile one can make people smile, too.

In this world we have the power to dream of anything possible, so let's relax the body and envision a wonderful world. Be aware of the breathing, while you are relaxing the head, this may give steadiness and grace to your being. Relax the body and breathe. The breathing is equally coming in and going out again. It is in one harmonious flow. The in-breath is our dear friend and the out-breath is our dear friend leaving us for a moment. Let's embrace this friend. Hello, welcome dear Breath, and Goodbye, dear Breath it is nice meeting you. The breath is always with us, saying hello for the space we are in and entering into the nostrils, streaming into the body. Within the body our friend enters our bodily kingdom.

It makes connection with our lungs, heart and other friends. The incoming breath is very well invited to also meet the belly. The belly is our common friend. Everyone knows the belly, as the friends meet together at the belly button, all the friends equally find themselves traveling back and forth, so the in-coming friend, the breath, now is saying hello to everyone, meeting and greeting the other friends, like the heart, the lungs, the belly, but also the cells and mitochondrion, as the breath can travel everywhere we can also meet the toes with the breath.

So the friends, aka tippy toe and the breath meet, greet and have a connection. This connection is very fragile and soft, so come, it can be even just spontaneous. When these meetings are done, the wonderful friendship parts and the beautiful journey goes on. So the breath says goodbye, I will see you, and then travels back from the lungs, over the nostrils into the space again: where we call this exhale. In the Space the breath is free to be.

From here, we are noticing the friendship and we are aware of the breath and with every single breath one can relax, or energize. However one likes. Now, as the we like to focus on the imagination, we just relax the body, so we are sure, not to float away. Balanced and safe we are grounded and relaxed, with the breath. The breathing goes in and comes out again, and we notice that the inhale is equal to the exhale, just fine and balanced.

The balance spreads around the whole body and we become lighter and lighter. We are becoming so light, we start to sink into our wonderful world of imagination where we can sit in a garden of friendship. This Garden of Friendship is free for us to be. We can invite all our friends or we can just sit in serenity. There is a nice cushioned grass patch for us, it is very soft and really inviting us for a meditation.

So we are sitting here, meditating with our bottom on the ground and we feel the soft grass on this lush field, there is also a tree, and we see, the tree greets us, too. Hello tree and beautifully the tree gives us shelter and a steady help to maintain peaceful and calm, this is what trees do, staying peaceful and calm. Beautiful isn't it? The tree is obliged and greets us with a smile, we smile back.

We are all breathing the same air, and look up into the air, there was just a fresh rain shower and now the sun comes along again, what a wonderful surprise the moisture in the air and over the field creates a haze where the sun shines through and there we have a glimpse of a multicoloured rainbow, shining and bowing to us, oh Hello, dear friend, I am the Rainbow; Welcome!

The rainbow bows at our feet and we are just seeing a lovely rainbow, that invites us with many beautiful colours, tender red, and golden orange, shiny yellow, bright green, light blue, indigo, and violett. All the colours are now with us, greeting us one by one, always bowing and Saying, Hello I am indigo, Hello, I am golden Orange, Hello, I am bright Green; and everyone smiles and we smile back.

The rainbow welcomes us for a walk and we can walk with the rainbow to see, where does this rainbow come from, yes, we Can show you. I am coming from the source. I am a rainbow born from the light, and born from the wonderful world. Here in this world you only see my seven colours, but in the imaginary world, the spiritual plane, the world is endlessly filled with abundant colours. There is no limit to the colours, as long as you can imagine you can also envision them. The colours I show you are within you right now, says the rainbow, and are coming out from this source.

We are standing on the side of an infinite pool, opening many beautiful layers of colours, it is a fountain, that springs with facets, oh friends, have you ever seen? This is the source of the rainbow, and it is beautiful.

The source seems to never end, and always creates itself from new. As soon as we think of a colour; indigo, indigo, indigo, the fountain becomes alive with this colour and we can also imagine forms, balls, flows, triangles and the fountain gives out many forms and shapes. It is a vision of the imagination, the eyes are ready to receive a wonderful gift of the mind. In our material world, the physical plane, only so much colours can be perceived, but within the dreamy, imaginary world, there is space to also free ourselves into more space. Space means the possibility to perceive more than meets the eye.

Oh, let's wonder why, the rainbow is coloured like it is,
anyway, the source is a source of bliss,
It springs endlessly coming into life, full of happiness.
The divine nature, the rainbow and the discovery is what it is.

Let's invite a friend to come with us on this imaginary world discovery, where everything is possible and let's say: thank you to the rainbow and the tree. What a wonderful harmony, this can be. Imagine yourself with the dearest of your friends, and invite this friend dearly; like the breath. One shall come and enjoy the imaginary paradise, as well as the gardens of friendship.

For a walk into the night, one can make it feel alright. Let's again envision the forms and shapes and know this is all here to be, our friend is now with thee. See, your dearest friend, heartily and kind, smiling, appreciating this friendship. Let's embrace this friend with all the colours of the rainbow. With all the love and devotion, with all the happiness and joy. Let's smile and find ourselves guided by the light, even in the darkest night.

Let's remember once more the beautiful discovery in this garden of friendship and how all the beings can be friends, peaceful and calm like the tree, in colourful serenity, the tender red, golden orange; shiny yellow, bright green, light blue; indigo and violet: all are here for friendship and for life, like the breath, making one feel alive. All the parts of the body are now in connection, in peace and serenity. There is now wholesome balance and harmony, from the tippy toes to the head, as are full in rest.

May All the beings be happy and free, in the colourful world of harmony,
May my friendship be with all, all the beings may be friends,
May the love and peace surround the whole world for good life.

May there always be light, even in the darkest night,
May our happiness and joy shine bright even in the darkest night,
May we greet the moon and the stars with a smile,
May ones happiness last for a while:

May all the beings be safe and sound, in peace, in love and harmony.
May I come back to the breath and to the body,
To fully engage in the life right here, right now. Chant and be happy.

I am the light of the world:
I am the light of the world;
I am, I am; I am the light of the world.

You are the light of this world,
You are the light of this world;
you are; you are; you are the light of this world.

We are the light of this world, we are the light of this world, we are we are, we are the light of this world.

May all be friends; may all be the light, even in the darkest night.

Parents Story

<u>1460 words, 20 minutes</u>

Once upon a time there was a family, that lives in the forest by the river stream. It is a sacred valley in midst the hills, where the family has a small lot for their cows and crops.
The family is a large family with 6 children, 3 boys and 3 girls. The peace of the lot is due to its nature, growing up on a land that is very safe and sound. The parents of the family are quite happy. As the work is benefitting, the nature is kind,u the crops are growing and the cows are giving milk. Around the lot there is a large forest and after the work is done the family enjoys together at the nearby stream. Cool and fresh water is running from its source just steps away, hidden in the forest.

The forest is a sacred one and the trees are as old as the family tree. When the young children come back from playing in the forest they enjoy a soothing evening with all the family members reading stories and playing music. The father of the family is the one who holds dear a very thick book, layered in leather. This book holds all the stories from the family as well as memories. In this thick book called the family tree book, all the leaves are filled with stories and every single evening, one is ready to read, a new story.
The father begins to tell the story of himself as a cowherd boy who gently and mildly plays the flute to soften the cows.

As the cows are grazing, the sound of the flute is also attracting the cowherd girls who are very tender and soft-skinned. They are maidens of the barn and equally share their work, bringing milk from the cows to the village where everyone shares the milk.

As one day I was playing my flute, says the father in a light voice, the cowherd girls came around to witness the scene seeing the cows joining in for a MOO and they start to laugh, one of them, even came to me, listening very closely. Attentively she looks at me, and there I knew, love is like a spontaneous flash that travels through all my veins and I became so devotionally encircled, to play the most beautiful melodies
.

The father looks over his reading glasses into the eyes of the children, like he always does, and there he sees the first member of the family already falling asleep. He smiles and continues in the book and reads on. This is how I got to meet your Mother, in this old memory I still find my love for her, and the love for the music remains.

Playing music is like embracing all the beings, because sometimes when Mother listens so kindly, the cows started to be amused with envy, they moo'd so loud that I didn't hear a word, but that just showed me, they feel for me, too.

Of course Mother was still so very young and we were rather happy to roam around the forest and play with each other, dancing and singing with the birds. While I was hiding in the tree I witnessed the wonderful cow maidens washing their clothes in the river just here and when they were bathing inside the river, I was sneaking down, hiding the clothes in the trees. When the maidens came out, they were in wonder where in the world would these washed clothes go? They could not walk from alone, but as I am a gentle soul, I gave them hints with my flute. Playing and making sounds to guide them into the forest to let them seek the clothes, of course I did not make any play with your Mother, because she knew who was playing the flute and was not in wonder.

Sitting up in the trees she glimpsed at me and I fell into her hands, she then got me and pushed me into the group of maidens who all saw me with my flute, I could not help myself, instead to play a song for them all and surely so sweet and tender they all forgave me. This song I still remember to this day.

Your Mother and I, we became very deep friends and sooner or later she met me alone, on a cool summer night, we were just sitting in the swing, swinging up and down enjoying the moon light. It was all in private secrecy but we enjoyed the beautiful moment. In these moments I can spot every detail, even every breath and it makes one so happy, I love to tell you more. Looking over the glasses, the next child fell asleep, very soon the father answered with a smile. What a surprise, the story goes on and comes around with a lesson.

Having family is to trust oneself and the partner. It is to obey and follow, and also to serve in devotion and love. As we all loved to dance, we organized dance gatherings in the forest, just lit with the light of the moon, the community was always very happy to hear my flute and to come together. Everyone was dancing, swirling around in circles following the beat of the drum. The rhythm got us and we continued deep into the night, while we were wearing our most elegant dresses. The parties were without any intoxication, we were just in happiness by moving and dancing.

When I got to dance with Mother the spark ignited a sacred flame that burns until this day, it is the flame that tenderly warms me from the inside and helps when I feel cold. Even in the cool night, the movement to the rhythm, looking into Mothers eyes feels like a warm shower.
From the sky sometimes dropped rain in and we all had to hide somewhere, of course I was hiding the best and could smile when I found another hiding spot with her maiden friends, I ask them, come on and dance along in the rain.

The rain dance could not extinguish the flame of excitement and joy within me, dancing with Mother in the rain, so in love and devotion; to the rhythm of the beat of the drum. Always following the next great adventure, we got together finding a dry spot at our home; in a safe nest, with a warm oven, making some tea and enjoying the smells of incense and herbs.

We just hold on here and continue next time, the Father looks over the glasses and another one was sleeping already. Then sooner enough, Mother comes into the room with a warm milk and Father closes the Story book. It is about that life, coming to ease, listening to stories, dancing and finding harmony. Love is like the honey in the milk that gives it a special taste.

Tender and sweet it awakens our senses and one feels a sense of life. To be alive means to love, love means to live. Aliveness comes from the union of our beings, sometimes even in a dark night, we can smile and shine bright. All families are unique and one of a kind, this is why we shall thank and appreciate every moment to feel alive. The family is also like a tree, bringing flowers and fruits to flourish and blossom. When the fruits are ripe and the flowers blossom they give us a special nectar, that when ready, is like honey, too. We are like bees enjoying this nectar and essentially bringing it back
Home into the Hive. Here the family resides and dances, and comes together in unity. Let's celebrate our harmony.

For once the family father pulls out his flute and plays a soothing good night lullaby, as Mother sings her favourite phrases from a book:

Like a light that stands still in the wind, the one who listens to the music of the mind, meditates and finds the ease, please,
Bring us harmony and peace, please bring us harmony and ease.
Together we are meditating and doing our deeds, raising a family, planting a tree, creating a life and living in harmony.

Whatever comes, whatever goes, one is steady in action and mind,
Let's unwind into a good, good night.

The play softens and fades, the family shuts the lights, yet is happy in harmony into the star-sprinkled night.
Let's find relaxation in every breath and continue to equally relax the body,
While breathing in and out, equally the rhythm of the breath goes.
We just follow along in the everlasting song, of life and light.
Following with a peaceful rest and a balanced state of mind.
Sleep, rest and relax.

Turtle Story

<u>1486 words, 20 minutes</u>

There once lived a wonderful Turtle named Kurma, Kurma the Turtle, is a wise and wonderful being that lives together in peace and harmony with its family. Kurma one day swims in the vast ocean of experiences to gather a glance if everything is alright. In the ocean of experiences it sometimes happens that there is a fight, and Kurma the wise turtle knows to bring long-lasting peace into the waters.

And there we go, two crabs are in a harsh discussion who is the harder shell, and eventually Kurma bears to wait until the long discussion ends, yet Kurma has much time and patience. The crabs, are now just wondering what is this wise turtle doing here. Is it listening to us? Kurma smiles and yes, Kurma listens and knows you two have an argument that ends no where, as eventually one or even two of you might be graced to be a nice conch shell for Neptune's orchestra. The Turtle smiles and sees the crabs in wonder. Neptune? Conch Shell? Who are you!

I am Kurma, to bring peace and long-lasting harmony into the waters and all life matters to me, it matters to me, because we have all the responsibility to keep the waters safe. The sound of Kurma soothes the crabs. Who is fighting who is harder is not relevant as all shall pass, and the ocean will maybe leave some sand behind, even the wisest and oldest turtle knows that. The crabs are baffled and start to ask, so please, wise turtle, what is the meaning of life? Kurma knows to be a happy helper and suggests to find it out themselves, yet he knows what is it not:

Either Hard, nor Bold, whether strong, nor stark,
All shall pass with a happy spark,
As a drop falls into the ocean,
We are all here just a moment in time,
We are like a breath, coming to go.
As the waters flow, fleeting in life.
Our only meaning is to be alive.

What does it matter, let's enjoy the time, to live a life, to ignite and spark the night. Every being is illuminating by a breath. Let's come together and celebrate. Kurma knows the crabs are wonderful musicians playing the hand drums, yet they waste their lives in fight. Play and let's have a good time.

Kurma leaves the crabs and invites them for a good night party, celebrating the kingdom of the underwater sea. Neptune shall come to have a party, personally. The crabs are happy to enjoy, coming along for the party and a song.
Under the sea, we found the meaning of Life, thanks to a turtle so wise, let's live a life!
Let's live a life in serving, doing the best we can, to enjoy every moment.
The crabs are happily clapping their hands and cheering. Happy Days, ending the fights, coming on a way.

Of goodness and harmony the Turtle continues to seek out the seas and bringing peace to thee. Kurma never forgets his family and therefore first comes back home, where everyone is delighted to see, Kurma helped another day of peace in the sea. The Sea is sometimes wild and a pool of meaning and ground. This is why the waves are making such a sound. Kurma comes home and enjoys the waves of tranquility and serenity.

Here we are breathing with the turtles, swimming in the sea, let's find a vessel, and we are ready to dive deep, there is no discussion as the turtles know to turn anger into music, we all can be a part. Let's enjoy the goodness of the sound, anyway, we trust, breathing and trust. A protective shield around the body relaxes the Self, Kurma invites us to come home.

We are seeing the ancient turtle almost growing larger than a car, with precious fins and a smile that is of many worlds worth. The turtle knows the sea so well and comes to live a life in simplicity. What a surprise the wondrous sea allows for a guest like Neptune and thee. The party never stops as the waves come to shore, we are all here to adore.

Whoever has a question can come to Kurma for advise, so sometimes the king of the sea comes to help with thee, Kurma please, how can we solve all the worlds unease? Kurma thinks about the Kings question and extensively looks around. The wise Turtle sees no problem though it hears a sound, I am just a child of this sea, as we are all a big family. No one is better than others and no one is greater than another, no one is richer or more wise than others. Kurma admits, I am not wiser than you, only you yourself, can know what's true.

Inner truth comes from experience, by breathing we know.
The body, mind and soul all come together with the help of the breath, the energy flows and can elevate all the sorrows of this world. We can be happy, we are alive,

breathing and making a life. Let's embrace that. Let's not seek any fight, let's not seek any strive, all is alright, right here and now.

From afar a loud conch shell sound illuminates the talk. Kurma grins and knows it is time to celebrate the sun set. The king bows and comes to show his gratitude, you shall be on my side, while I am here. Come along, to sing our favourite song.

Kurma smiles and adds, only as I can bring my family. The king bows in gratitude and allows the whole family to come. Let's all dance and have fun. The little baby turtles are there, the smaller young turtles are there and the turtles are all sitting next to the king. The king is delighted and joined by the crabs who are playing their drums now in the orchestra. The whole underwater community joins around the square and this is where the mermaids and merman tone the conch shells again.

This sound of a deep: WUUUHHH invites all the Dolphins, Whales and friendly Sharks. They are all dancing with the songs of the drums, from left to right and right to left. In circles and up and down. The singing whales are giving a show and the Dolphins like to blow water from their holes. The sharks are continuing to dance and the others gaze and see, the whole water kingdom is in harmony.

The golden rays of the sun are beaming on the surface and the sky is turning into colours of splendour and grace, all are happy to lastly see the suns face. Kurma smiles and is happily surrounded by his family. He whispers to his children. Do you see, everyone is in synchronicity, following the rays of the sun, dancing To the beat of the drum, yet we are here and witness all that, do you see? This is what a king can be.

Seeing this world in peace, love and harmony is a dream and therefore can be real, all matter comes from the unknown worlds of mysteries. So splendid the sun shines all mysteries are dissolved and infused with light, as soon as it sets, the night reveals the dream. Every dream can come true, we just have to believe and trust the whole, the whole of us, is dreaming a collective dream, flowing in a constant stream.

One knows the rivers that spring from a source, life unfolds and the dream flows on and on and into the sea, where eventually, after long lives, comes to shore. This is the way of the water and the earth, feel obliged and blessed that one is here.

Into the night without a fear, let's all be kind and listen to what one says, even may it be the moon, shining our way, telling a story of far galaxy's and universes.

Just listen to the sound and hear your breathing coming in and out, listen in and one is found.

It all starts with a humble seed,
Listen and repeat, follow the wise,
Come to ease and find the wise in you.

Make it a deed and be fascinated by life,
Wonder what it is, always curious and in bliss.
Happiness is all around us, can you see? Smile and be happy.

Kurma smiles and greets for a good night.
Let there be light even in the cool, dark night.
Let there be ease and peace, rest and serenity.
Let there be peace, love and harmony.

All equally, like the breath, in and out, coming and going, we are just breathing and happy to be alive, just happy to be alive. Relax yourself, fully breathing in and breathing out again. The breath comes and goes, and we ease with every single one.

Slower and finer, into the night, sleep well and rest.

Long life story

1492 words, 20 minutes

Once upon a time there was an eternal flame, burning for a long life. This flame was very well protected, guarded and kept safe. This flame was burning in the past and in the future, it is now present in every being. It is the everlasting flame of all love and of all life.
While we Breathe, This flame is transforming all the energies. As we breathe this fire is alive and flickering. To maintain this flame is to know the breath. This flame is sacred and also has a personality. It lives, flickers and dances in the wind, the wind is the everlasting play friend of the flame and the two are like best friends always finding a way of expressing themselves.

One is fully happy and in lust & laughter, that's the flame, one is harbouring the warm feelings of welcome home, that's the warm flickering flame of love and devotion. Flickering and dancing to the sounds of music, that's the joyful flame. All this is the same light, like the sun is equal to the sun light and the personality in the sun. The personality in the flame is called Agni, Devi or Goranga, shining in a golden bright light, the flame is always kept by the keepers. The keepers are also the keepers of wisdom who know the secrets of a long life.

Together we can all maintain our flame, and of course we can give our flame a personal name. The name of your flame might be different, yet it's one and the same. Like the rays of the sun is the same as the sun planet. Everyone can understand that.

Let's find this wonderful flame within our body and feel into it. It is very important to also know, that flames can transform a banana into a body. It is the flame that sparkles and sprinkles within our belly and it is the wonderful flame of digestion. This flame has many occupations, always busy and working tirelessly to
Maintain life.

So what does a flame need to steadily burn? Hm, it always needs a ground, because the flame has only so much space. So let's imagine a nice and beautiful space, like a shrine, an altar, maybe a safe fire pit, or even a tiny, tiny space as large as a candle light is also sacred and perfect for a flame. Agni doesn't matter how big the fire is, as long as it burns.

So, we close our eyes and imagine a wonderful flame within our dreamy world, in a sacred place. This place shall be totally serene and peaceful.

We can now sit by this sacred fire and find ourselves just knowing the guards are here to protect. A shimmer of golden light surrounds the sacred fire place. It heals, warms and nurtures our being and we find the fascinating sparkling of the flame speaking to us:

Oh Welcome to the inner fire that is here for you, I serve you as friend, fiery in nature I am willing to make the best happen, I can also transform a banana into a body's fuel. Let's embrace this moment and thank each other for the meeting. As we breathe, we keep the fire alive, just breathe and keep the fire alive, alive and alive, with every single breath.
So, we sit at the fire place, and we breathe, it also smells of smoky wood and the scent is making us feel warm and nurtured.
The peaceful flame chants a song:

Like a candle in a place of serene shelter, where no winds blow, I am here to show that life is light, dancing into the night, nurturing the sight and making eyes bright. I am to meditate with you, for a long life, letting one know, there is an easy way, one can practice every single day.

Let's meditate.

Inhale and Exhale, equally in and equally out again. See yourself in a sparkling shiny light, of devotion and love. See this light from the middle of you heart expanding into every cell of the body. This shimmering shiny light, shines from ones heart into every cell of the body. We become engrossed in shining light. We breathe and see ourselves in this light, just witnessing the beauty of it. The beauty of this light is in the heart, full of love and longevity.

Hold the breath in an equal rhythm, equally in, breathing through the nose and equally out again, letting the air go from the nostrils. The air streams into the body and helps inner life to move. The air is movement and with the breath the light can also move. The air travels with the light. See yourself protected with a beautiful glow, one is so safe and protected.

Now just keep the breathing equal and know everything is alright. The breath is moving in and out, the air constantly travels and we keep our senses to joy and happiness. Let's imagine a wonderful flame, the eternal flame of life, and we see it shine bright. Now let's invite a friend or family member to embrace this flame with us. It is a unique gift of life and we can share this present with the world and the loved ones around us.

When we breathe together, one can come into harmony. When we breathe under a tree, we come into harmony with that tree, when we come to breathe in synchronicity with a person, then we can come into harmony with that person. So let's unite with a friend or loved one and see that the breathing is nice and equal, harmonizing with the one.

Let's harmonize with all the world and see ourselves breathing life into the world. With every breath there is life streaming into the world, even the underwater beings and beings in the sky are breathing, somehow we are all connected with the air.

Let's celebrate this connection and find our friends and loved ones with us, so we can cheer the fire of celebration. The life flame dances and we sing songs of union. Let's pray and sing together.

Life is meant to be lived, dancing, chanting, in harmony.
Life is like a flame, playing in the wind, always enlightened,
Let the Light shine,
With a smile,
Let the love shine,
For a while,
Invite all you know,
Celebrate and show,
Affection and Love

The devotional flame dances and the sun goes down, but even in the darkest night, there, visibly shines a light. Light is also with us in our hands, the hands emanate healing light of love and therefore can heal. Our vision and eyes are connected to fire and the light, receiving and experiencing. Put your palms together in front of your heart, pray, and let a soft smile come onto your face. Now, run your palms together and see how the energy comes from the palms of your hands, getting warm and energized the hands are now ready and fully loaded.

Open your palms and close your eyes. Put the warm hands onto the face, so they can enlighten ones eyes. Breathe into the warmth and hold still for a moment, witness the light streaming from your hands into the eyes and into the body again and again. Breathe, calmly in and out, equally, in and out. As we feel, just remain in balance, breathing and maybe trying it another time, maybe now one can open the eyes to even see the lights streaming from the hands into the eyes.

Let there be healing light flowing, this energy is just like a soft sun, inside our hands. The soft sun, shining from our hands finds a partner in the eyes who are receiving. There always needs to be a giver and one who receives. Let's now open the palms into the air, gently breathing and concentrating on the heart. Imagine a beautiful golden light in between hands and heart. From one hand to another, to the heart, there shines a healing light of longevity.

May this light be with me,
May this light be with you,
May this light be with all.

Repeat,

May this light be helping me,
May this light be helping you,
May this light be helping all.

Repeat,

May this light be truth
May this light be love,
May this light be peace.

Let's imagine this light streams with the breath, in and out, coming and going. Rising and passing, just like the breath comes there also comes the night, and even in the night we are breathing, light, feel alright and notice the soothing melody of the own breath, this is life.

Give thanks and appreciation to all the loved ones around you and find yourself happy, and smiling. Smile gently and give this smile to your friends and into the night. May this smile by the light. May All have a good night, let's feel alright,
Sleep, Rest, and Relax.

Fire Story

<u>1504 words, 20 minutes</u>

Once upon a time there was a wonderful kingdom, with a King named Orin and the kingdom was very beautiful and always lit, even in the night there were candles burning to illuminate the community square, the treasury and the kingdoms temple. Some people in the kingdom were even walking in the night along the paths that were lit with candles because it looks so beautiful.

This kingdom was a fire kingdom, there all the people and even children were wise with fire. It so was their work and life purpose to keep the fires of the world alive. Fire is not just a flame for them, but for the fire kingdom it means a sacred life, burning and transforming the energies of the here and now.

Fire gives warmth and light as it receives energy from the wood, or other materials. Therefore the fire kingdom was also a wood forest, so they had enough to maintain the fire. In a beautiful setting by a stream, of crystal clear water, one might know that within the water is also a little bit of fire and vice verse. When you see a flame, there is also little shimmer of water in there, that's why water is necessary for fire. Also all of the elements are connected with the wind or air.

So there was a visitor, he came from the air kingdom and the fire kingdom was very obliged to receive a guest, for tea. Heating water over the fire, the temple president of the fire kingdom receives the guest with joy, what a delight to see you here, it must have been a long journey from the high realm of the air kingdom. There are four air kingdoms, but there is only one fire kingdom, as the guest smiles he answers, it is always a pleasure to visit you and see if everything is alright, any fight or stress lately?

The temple president of the fire kingdom looks around, just the usual, we have now a better treatment for unhealthy fights and struggles, we let them play drums and other musical instruments to relieve the tension, you might be able to see them, as there is a parade on this occasion to celebrate the birthday of the kings daughter.
Everything is set with a nice walking orchestra, across the city and you are well invited to join the ceremony.

When the tea was ready the temple president takes a sip and smiles, ah, this tea is a remedy for anger and lust, it helps to digest and makes you easy to rest. What is it asks the air man, it just a cup of love, filled with herbs from the garden, I shall show you.

What we can do make the inner fire smooth is to let loose and enjoy a moment with a friend, let's breathe and relax, let's smile and meditate in the garden of the fire kingdom. We walk along the path where sacred lamps light the way, flowers are standing here and there, bees are buzzing and the butterflies are in a flight. We love to see them play, so easy and tender, mild and happy. The fire president walks along an orchard, here and these are best summer fruits, they help for a good inner fire.

One can see almond, walnut and chestnut trees, as well as oaks and oh there are pIneapples growing, and coconuts, also apples and peaches, plums and oranges. We love the citrus fruits says the temple president because they bring good health to our fire. Let's find the best fruits for you and you might take them with you.

The fire president smiles and brings a basket of the best and hand-selected fruits, well ripened and juicy in nature. Life is precious like a wonderful sweet fruit, so full of juice and sept, the fluid that makes us feel alive. Inside on can also find the growth, within fruit that holds seeds, the offsprings for procreation. Nature is beautiful as such fruits grow from alone, just by the power of the sun and rain.

The air friend looks in happiness into the basket and smiles, what a great gift that is but I can not accept, I must be light, for my journey back. No problem, we will send it to you, and we will pack some more for your family. With red cheeks and a grin the walk goes on and the fire and air people are walking towards the procession, that goes on in honour for the daughter of the king.

One can hear loud drums and cymbals, beating in the rhythm of an ancient chant. These hymns are especially designated for the kingdom and the heirs, they shall show the power and grace of the worlds fire. Fire is here to keep and too many have forgotten to make a fire. We here have schools that teach how to make a fire and also how to be good fire bender, because fire is a powerful thing. In the Right hands it can heal and nurture, but wild, it is unimaginable difficult to handle. That's why we have controlled the fires, yet the children also learn to handle wild fires, which sometimes occur.
Under the guidance of a teacher we can then control and eliminate these.
It is an art, one can learn.

Within the parade there are also young children presenting a wonderful fire show, stunning in nature, fire is a fascinating element isn't it? It dances and flickers, it can be controlled and it can be wild, it can help the world to heal and grow. Wherever there is fire, there are also waters that flow.

There must be water, because without water and air, there is no fire. Yet, there can be light. This is why we also like to meditate with the sunlight, let's go here onto the hill, where we have a glance of the celebration under the setting sun.
The fire and air benders are sitting comfortably for meditation and it happens to be in a serene place, a little off the stress and noise of the parade, which is in full swing.
The sun sets.

Imagine yourself breathing the sun light. With every breath, there is sun energy streaming into the body and streaming out again. With every inhale we feel the sun light streaming into the body and we feel. After we let go, and the energy from within the body can stream out and be free again. Do this and just see, the wonderful golden light of the sun surrounding your body, as the sun shines from the inside of ones solar plexus, the sun also surrounds us. From within and from outside, there is wonderful, shimmering light. Powerful in nature, yet with the air and with the breath, being still and equal we can be aware of the light.

Sometimes sensations arise, like tickling, vibrating, or throbbing, but that's just the orchestra playing in the distance, we are here and now we are safe and protected with the sun light. The eternal fire of the sun also shines from within us and we are keepers of this sacred fire, while we smile, the light can come through and come out.
Sometimes one needs a spark, of that joy and happiness and when we see someone smiling it ignites the fire of life, love and laughter.

Let's just laugh together and make our belly bounce, it is very healthy, just like that. HA HA HA, HO HO HO, HI HI HI, HE HE HE, HU HU HU and the belly bounces and we have to hold our belly's so one can feel the belly bounce, again, HA HA HA! HO HO HO! HI HI HI!HE HE HE! HU HU HU! It is not necessary to always have a reason, but laughing and smiling is always healthy in nature, one can relax and let tension dance away.

The serene moment of happiness and laughter remains peaceful and we watch the night come in, the darker the sky gets, the more colourful the sky becomes and eventually the candles and lanterns are on, enlightening the city.
There is a beautiful process going on at the stream where young students praise the holy river and sway big oil lamps from left and right and into circles. The daughter of the king is very happy and delighted.

We are now safe and sound, in our personal space of light, finding our body and finding our breath, as we equally inhale and exhale the rhythm is smooth and in balance. Our whole body is in balance and we feel the inner flame smoothly burning, within. The stars are sprinkling and the moon shines its cooling light on the earth and into
Our hearts. We are very thankful for our own bodily kingdom and we remain peaceful and equanimous, in harmony and balance.

Let it be light, even in the darkest night.
Rest, Relax and Sleep well.

Salamander Story

<u>1491 words, 20 minutes</u>

Once upon a time there lived a fearless salamander, Salam, who was so fierce Salam could walk through the fire without a problem, actually people who saw it, also say, that Salam was even becoming one with the flame, not even burning or hurt, but totally save.
One with the Fire, yes. And Salam smiles, like nothing happened. It is the nature of a salamander, having practiced life long breathing and meditation, Salam is so relaxed, it just feels warm and comfortable.

One day another Salamander came to Salam to learn, and also this Salamander could do the same. Salam says, practice makes perfect and with the right breathing everyone can love the fire, and live in the fire. Some birds are up in the air, conquering the wind, some fish are under the sea, some animals are living in the soil, and I am nothing special, I am just thankful for the little bit of life.
The Salamander family is very humble and shy. Yet, Salam is out-going and preserves ancient breathing techniques that help one to stay calm in the fire.

Let's come into the place where Salam lives, to have a glance of a true devotee of the flames.

Hello, friend of the fire and curious Traveller! We are here to embrace the breathing and the fire alike, as all fire needs to be maintained with the air, the life force, as I call it. It is the wonderful power within every being. A turtle breathes and breathes very slow, that's why turtles get so old, Salamanders on the other hand breath very intense and quick and therefore we are able to maintain peaceful, in any heated situation.
Also we don't have a heater in our homes, because we are always warm.

Let's come to my favourite place, it is a hill, also called a volcano. But for that we have to step upwards into the hills and up the wonderful and mysterious mountains, Laka, that is the name of the volcano. Laka was here way before anyone else and therefore possesses true knowledge of the air and of course of the inner heat, inside the earth. Inside the earth, there is a core that is so hot, all the masses of rock and metal are fluid, because everything melts together, inside the earth, this core sometimes has an opening, and this opening is sometimes a fountain, a geyser, or a hill, like a volcano.

Let's imagine a wonderful cone-shaped hill, open at the top. There is a huge crater, and inside there is boiling, and cooking hot lava. This stuff is not as small as Grandmas pots, yet it is of the same intensity. The boiling ingredients are just nature's, like the one in Grandmas pot. It is all natural. The Laka Volcano invites us and with the guidance of the Salamander Salam we learn to know about fire and volcanos. This is a steep climb, so one better prepares for the ascension.

Breathe in and out, through the nostrils and the mouth, make the breath audible and listen to the breathing, coming and going, equally in and equally out again. The breathing is coming and going, in and out again. We are now in balance with our goal, we are ascending to the volcano. Breathing and imagining walking over great lava rocks, here and there we have to climb but with the help of Salam we find the right way. It is all for us prepared and one is safe, guided by a trusty friend.

We are breathing and with every breath we can hear the wind blow and the more we ascend, the more intense becomes the breath, in and out, equally in and equally out. The volcano is hot and Laka steams with great respiration. The volcano has been alive more many millions of years and is now ready for us.
Are we ready, too?
Let's go and climb higher and higher, with every breath we are getting one step closer to the top. Keep on breathing, and surely we can ask for help, Salam, please, we are almost there Salam answers with hope in the voice. Breathing in and out, just remember always, equal, in and out.

The volcano is there, we are there and now with a last step make it onto the top, looking in the horizon with a smile! Salam is happy for us and we see the giant pot, made by nature. It really is stunning, the lava is golden orange and steams with great intensity. There are many Salamanders around that play hide and seek at the volcano. Yes, this is like a melting pot, says Salam, every Salamander loves to come here. It is like a sacred place for us. The underwater creatures have Neptune's kingdom, the birds have great trees and nests, the earth beings have caves and shelters, and we have Laka.

It is also interesting that the world just grow like this, from the masses of the earth, colliding, and there is the story of a fire king who was so great he stomped into the earth with his Danda, stick, and there we go, there was a hole, which grew to be a volcano, isn't that interesting. Wonderful stories are also around this Salamander who was the priest of the kingdom and brought his family here for a ceremony, and since then we are always celebrating the sunset over here, one can imagine how beautiful the sight is from the volcano over the ocean to the sun.

The world has many great treasure but this here is my favourite one. Now, let's embrace the moment and meditate together. Bring yourself into a comfortable position and don't forget to equally breathe in and out. It is a very easy technique for a cool breath and I always use it when heated up. This can relieve any stress and tension, too.

Let's prepare the position, are you comfortable and breathing, equally in and out? Yes, ok.
There is chance the tongue needs to be prepared because we are now rolling the tongue into the shape of a tube, both sides bending to the top of the base.
The tongue is like a straw and with it we are inhaling and exhaling cool and fresh air. Cool and fresh air is streaming through this tube, into the mouth and one is exhaling with the nose, are you feeling it? Cool and fresh, air breathing into the mouth, with the tongue straw sticking out, and breathing out through the nose. This is a wonderful technique, breathing in, through the mouth, with the tongue rolled inwards and out again, equally in and equally out again.
Wonderful, now let the breathing be normal and just see the sun setting into the ocean, like a great ball of light, going down to rest, tenderly sinking into the bed of the ocean. The Salamanders are chanting nice songs for the sunset:

Oh greatest fire alive, you sun light, so bright!
Let's embrace the change and transform the ways.
From the fire of old and the fine days,
Comes the new and also the night.

Let's celebrate the sight, let's unite within the light,
Let's breathe in harmony and find ourselves in unity.
All beings shall be happy and free, for eternity.
All beings shall be happy and free, for eternity.

This wonderful spectacle is happening everyday, says Salam, yet every time it is special, thank you for being with us and going up this hill of fire, where we Salamanders live. I appreciate and always like to join your way back down, let's ask a friend who is so eager to happily bring us to the home. A winged-Salamander is coming into our sight and Salam says, this is my wife Sally, she likes to bring you home, so you can rest in ease.

Let's embrace a goodbye to Laka and have a nice flight.
While we glide down on Sally's back, we see the ocean reflecting the last sun beams and the sky turning into beautiful colours, on the feet of the hilly land, where Laka resides.
It is a magical place says Sally and I know every time coming here to witness the transformation from day to night is something one-of-a-kind. Like you.
She smiles, we smile back.

Let's all be happy and smile, so all the beings may be in the light, of love, of wisdom, of light. May all the beings Be happy and free. Let's come home for a good nights rest.
We find the breathing again and the awareness travels back into the body. The whole body is fulfilled with a lovely experience from the fire land of the Salamanders, let's remember the best parts and keep surely sharing this story, into the night. As the light of life shines even in the darkest night.
Sleep well and rest.

Jungle story

Around the Island of the Laka mountains, in the middle of the sea, on a volcano island there is a Jungle with many great trees, long water ways and a happy Jungle kingdom. This kingdom always offers guests to come on a spiritual journey with the guides that are the friendly Ant, Anthony and the great, parrot, Patrick. Anthony and Patrick are a sweet duo, that unlike others never fights. They just laugh, or repeat each other, when there is difficulty understanding. The parrot loves to repeat, loves to repeat and therefore often comes around very funny, very funny. Yet, Anthony is never missing to laugh of his jokes.

Once a parrot was sitting high in the trees and Anthony thought it was Patrick, unaware, that sometimes Patrick's twin is with him. In a matter of a second he awoke and asked, why is this Ant on my nose? Anthony looks at him, and smiles, may I carry you down the tree? Down the tree? Yes, the sleep got me dreaming of very strong Ants that are able to carry Parrots like me, Parrots like me. Anthony, never ever minded and got his whole Ant family, which are quite a few and there they brought the slumbering Parrot onto the ground. Safely resting in the basin of a paradise island, the Parrot wakes up and is in total wonder, why is my twin making dinner again, was I not suppose to prepare, to prepare? Let's fly to meet my Family, totally still in his dreams Patrick forgot about dinner and starts to cook for the whole family, there comes Anthony and wonders why he is not sleeping in the basin of the Paradise, not sleeping in the basin of the paradise? May I am in disguise?
Let's come here and see, this is where I put thee, I put me?

There comes Patrick's twin ready to cook the dinner and Anthony wonders why he can see, double, any way, what's that for dinner, and what's that for a night? Anthony smiles bright, knowing to invite his whole family. It is time to celebrate and Anthony climbs up the whole tree with his family, we all are ready, is Patrick here, is Patrick here, the twin shows up, yes I am, yes I am, Patrick is Patrick and I am here. Are you all good with rice?
I don't mind, I don't mind. It sometimes all looks the same, as the Ant cannot See, the Parrot left his glasses behind and the whole family of the Jungle was fed that day.

There is a nightly festival, can you hear the drums? We Parrots sing, we Parrots sing and the Ant claps his hands. I know you do. Let's join the festival, let's join

the festival. Let invite all the family, all the family. The ants are gathering clapping and chanting the Parrots repeating the phrase.
Let's all be Happy,
Let's all be Happy.

In the World,
In the World,

Of sounds and joy,
Of sounds and joy,

And whenever we can sing,
And whenever we can sing,

One shall let it be,
One shall let it be.

Let's all be friends,
Let's all be friends,

In the World,
In the World,

sounds of happiness,
sounds of happiness,

And whenever we can be,
And whenever we can be,

One shall let it free,
One shall let it free.
Let's all be free,
Let's all be free,

In the World,
In the World,

Sounds of Harmony,
Sounds of Harmony

And whenever we can dance,
And whenever we can dance,

One shall let it be,
One shall let it be.

Let's all be family,
Let's all be family,

In the World,
In the World,

Sounds of unity,
Sounds of unity,

And whenever one can be,
And whenever one can be,

One shall be in harmony,
One shall be in harmony.

The parrot are chanting on and on and it goes on and on, like the Jungle never sleeps, there is always someone awake and singing or chanting, or dancing, or letting it free.
That's the nature of the jungle, Always alive, like the river streams and fountain always springs the jungle always sounds of peaceful harmony.

The trees and animals are all in happiness, dancing and singing, while the sun goes down and there comes the king with a beautiful crown on his head, enjoying the Sunshine and the sounds of peace, harmony and joy. The king is joyful himself and smiles while he waves, decorated with just a loin cloth.
He is very young and the kingdom loves to have a young king, as all the animals follow the guidance of the mountains, where Laka resides. The birds are following the guidance of the trees and the trees are following the guidance of the earth. The earth is represented by the mountains and the volcano Laka, around the hills, the volcano serves as a playground and for ceremonies as all the jungle inhabitants are coming together to sing and dance.

Life is unique in the Jungle, yet the sunset always comes and never fails, yet today there is a tropical storm which might come down, yet all the people and animals of the jungle are joyfully celebrating and even the jungle storms are splendid showers of warm rain. The wind today is just a little in wonder, it is like searching, where did I leave my keys? The wind is searching for touch and for contact, sometimes some more, sometimes less. This time the Jungle inhabitants love to soothes the storm by singing a heart full song for the storm and for the rain.
Abundant the jungle people show up to soothen the storm with their great instruments - all voices joining together and even the animal king of the jungle, the lion shows up with a furious ROAR. We can join in, opening the mouth and stretching the tongue out: ROAAAR! And again, all together ROAAAAR! The orchestra starts and the lion is in full swing, dancing his most favourite dance. The wind blows but then sees the lion even all the jungle inhabitants just showing up for the celebration, and to soothe the storm.

There comes a white dove and speaks: Yes, the storm comes in peace, bringing us just the finest of the rain, giving us again new water to nurture the plants and trees. To give us a shower, finally! May all be happy!

The storm clouds break and the rain falls in huge drops soothingly onto the heads of all the animals. All the party animals are now very calm and peaceful, just playing their natural songs of happiness and joy.

It rains,
It rains,
The storm is here,
Bring us joy,
And have no fear.

It rains,
It rains,
We celebrate the sight,
Even the sun sets,
Into the night.

Come here,
Come here,
Feel the light,
Breathing in,
And out, alright.

The storm clouds open and the rain tenderly diminishes into a fine sprinkle, whereas the clouds make space for the golden sun setting into the ocean with a surprising last sun beam the sun light and the water of the rain create a sky-full image in all colours.
Can you see the image?
All the colours in the sky,
Oh I wonder why,
We are so blessed,
With such a rain,
Giving us all relief,
From the pain.

Relax the body and prepare for a good and soothing night.
The endless coming and going of the winds is just like the breath, coming in and out, sometimes there might be a cloud, yet the light is always there, shining into the air.
The heaven is open and the breath is free, let it be, let it be,
Let it be,
All beings may live in harmony,
Happily and free,
Like the lion dances for the rain,
The whole jungle enjoys a sight,
Even when the golden sun sets,
Into the good good night,
There might be an image,
Of the whole world in peace,
Find the relaxation and ease.

Relax the body from the crown to the feet and welcome the stars on this beautiful night, there might be, the moon saying hello when the sun lights it face. Let's hope and trust, for our friends and family. Whenever we feel joy, like the whole jungle party in a blissful act, then one might think of the world, and the ones that can receive the joy.

Think of the friends and family and all surrounding you in light, shining even into the fresh and dark night. The jungle party never stops, like the life energy, is always with the breath. This connection ever lasts and helps us through the storm, find comfort even in midst the storm, with the breath, constant and steady.

Find peace within the breathing, because breathing means life, even in the good, good night.
Sleep and rest well.

Monkey story

<u>2006 words, 30 minutes</u>

Once upon a time, there was a monkey living in the Jungle with the name of Cameron and Cameron was a brave and smart Monkey who could climb up the trees to gather bananas and coconuts. The monkey lived well with his family as the jungle provided for everything. All was there for Him and his family.

Jumping left and right and back and forth the monkey had a curious sense of exploring. His mother always says, please be careful, we care about you. The monkey was listening and helped himself to find a comfortable spot in the hammock, where life was just swinging away. Watching the clouds in the sky move and travel, the monkey dreams of foreign lands where his other relatives are living. India, Thailand and Hawaii; all these places have monkeys and Cameron's uncle is just on his way back from India visiting the great city of Agra where the world wonder stands, the Taj Mahal.

Cameron's uncle arrives with a boat and around his neck is hanging a wonderful flower garland, what a surprise, he instantaneously jumps out with a bamboo flute and chants Hare Krishna Hare Krishna, back from India I bring happiness and blessings. He smiles, funny uncle, thinks Cameron and he asks him, please dear uncle can you tell us a story of the great land so far away?

Uncle is charmed and feels obliged to tell a story.
You know, we had a meeting in the great city of Agra and close to it there is the most famous travel destination for Pilgers, people who like to visit holy places, and there the monkeys are very wonderful, dancing and chanting, sitting on the river side and playing with the cows. The cow is also holy and Indians get food to feed the cow, but as soon as we visited, the markets full, the wonders started to happen.

The monkeys in this holy place are serving the best foods, because they are attracting the crowds. Unlike any other animal, here the monkeys dance and put foods on silver plates to bring it to the holy cows and saintly people. There was one older person, a very great personality with a white robe and many flower garlands, there were seven monkeys around him, bringing him this and that.

The monkeys here are wonderful and kind, serving only the freshest ingredients.

The freshest Bananas, one can ever find and what happened with us? We were so welcome, they treated us like a cow! Holy Cow!
The monkey laughs and climbs up a tree. Here, who wants my flower garland? He throws it into the air and Cameron still stunned by the fantastic story catches it. Please uncle, can you tell us another story? He throws the garland back to his uncle. Yes, of course. India is very rich in celebrations and people are singing and drumming on the streets, this is really amazing because it so so loud! But peaceful, there is no one, hurt or sad, everyone is happy and kind.

The fabulous experience of the celebration was a highlight and when one of the monkeys had a flower garland left, he said, maybe you find a dear devotee.
So, I did.

Stories here and there, but everywhere we go we can see how we are all one family. From the ancestors, our fathers the pre-apes, and now us monkeys living a life in paradise.
We are all of one family, and one can see that. Yet, we all like to chant and be happy, and we all like to celebrate with our friends in devotion.
Whatever the reason maybe, we all shall be happy!

I might tell a little more of the monkeys living around the great Palast, the wonder of the world. The Taj Mahal, they are funny but sometimes they are still very wild, playing in the water fountains and jumping into the pools, making each other wet and climbing up the coconut trees, to gather a fresh cool up. It is very warm on the Indian sub continent, but the monkeys don't mind, they are so engaged and happy, they even live in colder climates, up in the hills. We have so many stories to tell, what would you like to know?

How can you not live happily on this island? Uncle smiles and knows Cameron is a sweet heart. It is all possible, I can, but my monkey mind is always moving and I just follow the sense of exploration. I love the sea and there now, it is smart to make my life a living dream.

I know, my father always presented me his stories and always wanted to know, what is it about. He travelled extensively and therefore knew a lot of the world and of the people. Sometimes he even got me a present, a silver banana, I still have this banana, because it reminds me of all the stories. Here in the jungle, we have to live very closely together, I like the freedom like my father.

Freedom? Cameron doesn't know what that is, how can I be free?

Well, one can be free in many ways. Some likes to hang around and enjoy the endless sky, that's freedom. One can also move around freely, like going on a travel.
In between there infinite ways to be free, I'll let you know, maybe you like to sing and play?

Cameron is nodding, yes like everyone. Yes of course. Everyone likes to sing and play. Let's be free with our voice: UH UH UH, the monkey starts to sing:

Free in paradise, what a surprise!
I love the trees and the trees love me,
Free as a monkey.
I love the peace and harmony,
No car,
No house, no spouse, free as a monkey.

Uncle, are you really free? You need a boat, that brings you from one place to another!

Cameron, my dear, because there is the freedom of the wind, the boat can sail, we are just like a guest on board watching the sails set.

What have you seen, dear uncle, is it a good sight?

Cameron, you are my light,
That's why I always come back to home,
Because you are very dear to me.
Let's enjoy the beautiful island harmony.

But will you leave again?

My friend, it is in the space, where the wind blows and where we enjoy a breeze, together with the coming and going of the waves the journey always moves. That's why I am always on the way. Life moves, I move.

You say something with the Monkey Mind, Cameron is a very curious monkey.

Yes, that is within all beings, the humans have it, too. Do you know, when there comes a thought, oh I have an idea, and then somethings let's us let go of this idea and one comes into a dance, maybe I shall go here, or maybe there, or maybe here, the uncle shows with a finger in different directions. It is like you jumping from one tree to another tree. Yes, I am very good at jumping from one tree to another tree, Cameron smiles.

Yes, that's it, let's be happy and do what makes us happy. This is great, uncle, thank you.
Cameron smiles with affection and hops into a tree to find himself a coconut. Uncle looks at him and says, this must be CamConut, you wonderful Cameron, please let's make a song out of that.

Who over got a Coconut, is that You?
Find it Hanging from a tree, is that true?
So many questions and only one answer.
Yes, there is everyone ok, happy and harmony.

What if there is a Coconut, hanging from a tree.
May there be, a wild monkey, climbing up, reaching high,
And once we shake the tree, it falls on the ground, CLAP.
Let's make the sound, and know, why why why.

There is a tree for every fruit. So is everyone one of a kind,
There is a father and mother, even for the monkey mind.
Let's all unite in harmony, and set ourselves free.

Uncle, did you just make up this song?

Well, life is like that, always moving and in flux, spontaneous and new.
And before we knew, there is the chance to redo,

To learn and grow.

Uncle, what is the biggest lesson you have learnt on your travels?

It is the question I ask myself, too. Dear friend and nephew, Cameron, all the lessons are great. Learning to accept myself as a traveller and also accepting my home to always come back.
Let's find ourselves happy and in harmony, playing and the things we live and love.

There is no better and worse, just live a life of love.

Find the playful side of love and devote yourself to that, and when it makes you smile, then everything will be alright.

The monkey smiles and embraces Cameron.
It is nice to have you here with me, dear I am glad to be at home, equally, I am glad to go somewhere.

Remember the meditations I have brought you from Thailand?
Breathing in and equally out, equally in and equally out again.
This is like life, always changing, sometimes we climb up the tree, to fetch a coconut and sometimes one is finding a coconut straight on the ground. Lucky if it has fallen and opened up by itself. May we have a chance to thank our lives and devote our love to the world.

We can breathe and be happy just like that, with all we have, maybe one coconut a day is fine, maybe that's all we need. Maybe we can also live like Hanuman, do you know that the Indian Monkey King is the saviour of a whole kingdom, flying all over the sea to rescue the Queen. I may say that there is the chance to help and enrich the lives of others, this is how my father got this silver banana.

He was a servant of the empire and helped to prepare food, serving a long time and doing the best with his team. Together, the enjoyed also serving the others on big festivals. Because without someone serving, there is no deserving. One has to act according to ones destination and my father was the best server, he got to be honoured with this silver banana, personally from the king.

The king gave this banana to Him and he gave it to me. Isn't that fair, he receives it and presents it to me, now I am serving with this story to help others, like you and maybe when I am old, and cannot travel anymore, you can receive a present like this.

Cameron smiles and instantly thinks, oh now I can climb up this tree to have a banana, but not just for me, but also for my family.
The monkeys brings a whole batch of bananas to the ground, shiny and ripe.
Uncle says, yes, let's go home and bring it together to the family.
This night Cameron learnt to also share his bananas and coconuts, like his uncle is sharing stories, of all kind.

May all beings be kind to one another, may we all share this kindness and give it our friends and family. May all beings be happy, living in Peace, Joy and Harmony.

May, all beings be at peace, living in the happy unity, where no monkey mind springs from left to right, but we serve, as the family is resting, we are now resting, because relaxation and balance are the greatest gift of any being.
See the balance of a tree, a monkey, a bird.
Even sleeping, we can find balance and harmony.
May all beings be happy.
Say good night to the jungle family and have a wonderful rest, bringing a smile to your friends and family, serving with the joy and grace of a smile is always light, even in the darkest night.

Sleep well, and rest.

Rescue story

429 words, 7 minutes

There once was a kingdom in a beautiful land.
Rich and abundant this kingdom had a prince, ready to receive the crown. When he found a wonderful princess, the princess was just the perfect until she disappears. Like a curtain closes, the mystery remains and all the kingdom wonders where she is.

There is also a monkey family who are all watching the woods, and they help to find the coming queen. Like a silver beam a shooting star shot across the realm. The forest lighting up with a bright flash. A shooting star! The help is coming to rescue. The monkeys have a leader, Harmony, who is very wise and genuine. He says, yes I can save the Queen. She send a shooting star to us and we have to find.

She sent a shooting star? Yes, it is her writing and we have to go North to find her. It is the duty of monkeys to serve the kingdom and help with your search.
We can walk to the north to seek out the Queen. The prince is ready to find her and he and the monkey Harmony agree, to be on this mission. Harmony says, you wait here, to stay safe and in peace, prepare the Kingdom for the coming back of the Queen.
Harmony has super powers and flew across the lands to rescue the lady Queen, out of the island, where a coconut tree invited her to come. She was looking for the stars and when she suddenly stood still, she was mysteriously sitting on that tree, in total serenity.

Harmony, waking her up, says I have to rescue you and bring you back to the kingdom it is my duty to serve the prince. The queen smiles and sees the fire of devotion burning with Harmony and together both travel back to the kingdom.
Arriving back, the kingdom was relieved and together they could finally live back in serenity. Together they can enjoy the unity.

Let's imagine sitting under a tree, with nothing to fear, and the wonderful Harmony, coming in great fearlessness and devotion decorated with a silver crown and gems of precious stones hanging from his neck, with strong arms and rings set with Blue sapphires holding a hand to rescue. Everyone who is in fear just scream:

HARMONY! And with the help of the greatest devotee of the Kingdom, one shall come to be with you.

Together he gives us the advise to evenly breathe and be balanced, to any surprise, even in the darkest night.
Sleep, rest and relax.

Bird story

<u>448 words, 7 minutes</u>

There once was a forest, a kingdom and a natural reserve, where all the birds came to land and preserve. The birds are on a long journey from the lands far away and coming here everyday, is the sight of the a peaceful place, resting and nesting in this serene sanctuary.
The sanctuary is of a precious golden bird, who delivers messages for the whole country. Faster than any post can, in-time and always secret, this bird is the keeper of many mysteries.

From the beak and around the feather bed there hangs a little letter that flies with the bird to reach its destination. The destination might be far away, yet, the bird brings it anyway and always finds back home. A long, long time, after a journey. The bird rests in the nest and wherever he rests there is always a circle surrounding him with light, asking questions and finding the delight. In his sight, he knows many stories and has visited all the lands, from far to close.

Are we one of those?
Where is the most beautiful place?
How can I deliver on time?

Questions after questions and the golden bird just sings a song, whistling it all night long.

Hear the breath, coming in and going out, the soothing melody of life.
Relax and be content with who you are and you can follow the star. There is the chance, to embrace the timeless now, and one shall ever be ready, to deliver and to be in peace, love and harmony.

The ways of a messenger might be long, but surely bring your favourite song.

I am the light of the world
I am the light of the world
I am the light of the world

You are the light of the world
You are the light of the world

You are the light of the world

We are, We are, We are the light of the world.

Even in this forest and within this kingdom where a bird nests that brings messages to everyone, he always comes back, so a traveller from long, dreamy journeys always comes back, home, into the body with the breath.

Gently breathe in and out again, breathe and feel just fine, and align with the sky, with the sun and the sky, with water, fire and earth. Feel comforted and at peace, one is the light of the world. The world is an endless place of discovery, yet we all come back home.

Enjoy the message of the bird and find the breath, equally and in balance.

May this night be alright and may evenly our light shine into the darkest night, sleep and rest well.

Prince and Princess story

<u>770 words, 10 minutes</u>

There lived a Prince, who is genuine and kind, and he wants to establish a kingdom where all can be kind, so he gives everyone a work, a thing to do, and hence it becomes true, follow this way and once in a life the happiness will be your way.

For every given smile and every breath you do, you might receive the flowers and fruits, for every hand you shake and every present you give, one shall receive the shelter, with the feet one shall walk align and true, now the waters shall be with you.

Find the serenity even in the hardest storms and one shall be relived of any pains. Keep a steady mind and just be kind, just be kind.
The Princess hears him dear, and adds, one shall grow a family tree, of life and love. Having devotion for the here and the above. Honour the sky and the earth alike, find yourself in peace and relax every night with ease. May we be rewarded with the light of the moon and celebrate together in peace, love and harmony.

The Prince is standing on a pedestal and his Queen is next to Him. He whispers in her ears, without you I am just a normal person, human, like all the same, humble in devotion I became a prince to serve you. To treat the kingdom good for you. The love for the right way of ruling is just for the love of All. He tenderly smiles at her. Both are happy.

The Prince starts to chant a soothing mantra.

You are my moon light, you are the stars that shine bright. You are the one that is next to me, likewise no other can be.
I see in your eyes and tenderly melting is my heart. I am like butter, in the flame of your gaze, melting away. I become soft and at ease, all the pressure falls off and I can be.

When I look at all we have been through, from the forest, of the kingdoms, living apart, and coming back in serenity. Together we are strong, together we can sing a song.

Of Peace and Love and Unity.

Let's embrace the Harmony,
Prince and Princess on a Pedestal,
Marble and finely carved both stand tall,
Over the endless kingdom's sky
I have the answers why, why, why.
There is love, for one,
There is love for all.

May my love for you equal the love for everyone.
May my devotion to you, equal the devotion for all.
May all my blessings be with you and the world.
May all the grace fulfill the hearts of all.

You are my heart,
So tender and sweet,
You are the symphony,
The wisdom and grace,
Within, I find the space,
When I see your face.
There is this common phrase:
Let there be love,
Let there be light,
Even in the darkest night
May all beings be alright,
In Peace and equanimity,
And whatever may be,
We breathe, we come to thee.

The Prince looks up into the sky, do you ever wonder why we are here, he asks in a child like voice?

The Queen looks at him, as if there is all said, and still a wondrous gaze flashes into the air, while both look up there, comes a shooting star flashing by, like a great wish come true.

Lets find ourselves meditating in the Garden, lush and green. We see the Prince and Princess standing there. What would you do, which wish shall come true, seeing a shooting star, that could be you. Anything is possible, stay believing and trust the light, even in the darkest night.

Breathe and relax. Let all the stars shine and surround yourself with healing light of love.

Light and Love may shine from our Hearts to the whole world, so all beings shall be at peace. Hold this thought dear and find the smile, always smile, for your friends and family.

Smile in peace, love and unity.

Breathe and know, everything is coming and going, every Kingdom, every prince, every princess all are living a moment, that is special and unique, like every breath is unique, in and out it goes, notice how equal the breath is. Notice how calm and peaceful one can be.

Let it be, in peace, love and unity.

Into the night, sleep, and rest.

Fairytale story

<u>393 words, 6 minutes</u>

There once was a curious traveller, going from place to place, always in wonder, where is the magic, where does the story come true, where is the me and where is you?

There came a man, so humble and kind, with wisdom so long like his ears and his gaze was straight into ones eyes. Well, you search, and still search? Become the stillness and let search find you. Let it be.
The fairy tale is coming to you, just sit still.

The traveler stands still in awe and sits down, without a tone. His eyes are almost falling and as they are half closed he wakes up by a flash, in front of his eyes it must have a fairy. He gazes onto the nose, yes indeed! A fairy waves at me!

Welcome, you, met our Teacher who loves to fulfill the search and as you have been searching until here, you shall see, what a fairy world looks like. Wait here and close your eyes. Fully and Gently.

Let's be prepared, here comes the ferry dust.
Like flower petals so kind and soft falling unto the skin,
The ferry dust comes from the fairy world within,
In a sparkling source we can finally see,
There is more, so let it be,

Coming to the world of a wonderful possibility.
There sits the teacher in a shiny glow,
To the feet of a tree, and a flower to show.
Everything may be, and we can ask the wise,
What life may be, may be?
Will I be free, is there eternity?

The wise one with the gaze opening hearts, tenderly speaks from the heart. All is One, of a kind, in a rhyme, even in the sunshine, like this flower here, we can blossom and listen and feel. The flower rose and stands from alone, growing to be a wonderful hedge, I am the flower without a thorn, life is peaceful and we shall be born, every moment, breathing, fleeting like my scent, there is the sky the heavens tent.

Just lay there in wonder and let it be, it will come to thee.

The wise one, and the ferry and the flower wave for a good night and we shall find, all light, even in the darkest night.

May all beings be happy and free.
Light is eternity.

Sleep well.

Bedtime Stories For Kids 30 Day Challenge: 30 Days Of Guided Meditation & Fantasy Stories To Help Toddlers & Kids Fall Asleep, Relax Deeply, Develop Mindfulness & Bond With Parents

Mindfulness Meditations Made Easy

Contents

The Most Uncomfortable Bed in the World 2

The Elf With Incredibly Large Ears 7

The Most Beautiful Places in the World 11

The Baby Bird Who Fell From Her Nest 15

The Unicorn Who Lost His Tail 20

The Mermaid Who Couldn't Swim 25

The Four Little Pigs 29

The Princess and the Prince 33

The Trees Throw a Party 38

The Nice Dragon 42

The Wrong Potion 47

The Bee Who Loved All of the Flowers 51

Uncle Ron Babysits 55

When Aliens Attack 60

The Trapped Fairy 65

The Boy With No Birthday 69

The Baby That Could Not Sleep 73

The Weird Guy 77

How To Calm Your Mind 81

The Musical Animals 85

The Oil Fountain 90

The Most Beautiful Flower In The World 95

The Labyrinth 99

The Story Of Sleep 103

From Red To Green 107

The Wind 111

When The Moon Disappeared 115

The Luckiest Boy In The World 120

Survival 124

The Angry Crocodile 128

INSTRUCTIONS FOR AUDIO RECORDING: 20 MINUTES PER STORY FOR A TOTAL OF 10 HOURS.

THANK YOU!

The Most Uncomfortable Bed in the World

Once upon a time, there was a little girl. Her name was Alice, and she was four years old. The thing that she loved to do more than anything in the world was to sleep. When bedtime came, she would curl up in her bed as her mom and dad read her a bedtime story, and she would slowly fall off to sleep.

Well, she wouldn't slowly fall off to sleep. First, she would have to make herself comfortable, for her bed always seemed to turn into the most uncomfortable bed in the world as soon as she tried to make herself comfy.

"Are you comfortable?" asked her mother.

"I think so," said Alice.

Her mother opened the book and began to read the story of the elf with the big ears. She had only just read the first sentence, which was 'Once upon a time,' when Alice started to squirm in her bed.

"Are you okay?" asked her mother.

"There is something in my bed," said Alice. She wriggled around like a wriggly worm, flipping her legs back and forth as if she was as uncomfortable as she could get. Finally, she could take it no longer, and she jumped out of bed to try and solve the problem. Her mom and dad helped her to find what was bothering her.

"Perhaps it is a rusty, old nail," said her father.

"Maybe there are some rocks in your bed," suggested her mother.

The three of them searched through the bed from top to bottom and almost came up empty-handed. It was Alice who found the culprit.

"Aha!" she shouted as she held her and aloft. Her mother and father had to come closer to see what she was holding. There, between the tip of her index finger and her thumb, was a small piece of brown fluff. It was barely the size of a pea, and we all know that anything the size of a pea cannot make you uncomfortable, but it did make Alice uncomfortable.

Her mother and father frowned, but they were glad that the annoyance had been found, and, when Alice was back in bed, her mother once again started to read about the elf with big ears.

"Once upon a time," started her mother.

"Ouch," said Alice.

"My goodness, what is wrong now?" asked her mother.

"The mattress is sticking into me. I think that there is something wrong with it, maybe a spring is loose," complained Alice.

"Let's call your father to help," suggested her mother.

When her father came, they took the blankets and pillows from the bed, removed all of the stuffed toys (of which there were a lot), removed the sheets, and looked at the mattress. Alice's father conducted a thorough examination of the mattress, checking every square inch. He got in close so that he could examine the fabric, he ran his hand over the surface to make sure that nothing was sticking out, and he pushed down on the springs to check that they were still springy. They were.

"Looks fine to me," he said.

"Have you checked the other side?" asked Alice.

Her father frowned, but he knew that his daughter would not go to sleep until she was comfortable. They already had everything off the bed, so it would not take much more effort to check the other side of the mattress. When he lifted the mattress, Alice saw the problem immediately.

Under the mattress was a shiny, green pea. Alice picked it up and smiled. "This must have been bothering me," she said.

Her mother frowned and took the pea from her daughter. She knew better than to question how a pea could cause so much discomfort.

"Perhaps there is another fairytale that we can read," suggested her mother, inspired by the discovery of the small pea under the mattress.

"No, I like this one," smiled Alice.

The three of them worked to put everything back on the bed. The sheets were tucked in, the stuffed animals were put back in place, the blankets and pillows were laid on top, and Alice got back into bed.

"Are you comfortable now?" asked her mother.

"Oh, yes!" exclaimed Alice.

"Good," said her mother. She restarted the story of the elf that had large ears. "Once upon a time."

Alice fidgeted under the blanket, pulling it up around her neck, and then pushing it down to her chest. She flopped her arms in top of the blanket, and then stuck them underneath it. She moved her head from side to side on her pillow and sighed.

"Are you sure that you are okay?" asked her mother.

"Completely fine," said Alice.

"Okay. Once upon a time," started her mother.

"Hmph," said Alice.

"Once upon a time," said her mother.

"Hmm," sighed Alice.

"Once upon a time," whispered her mother.

"Grr," said Alice exasperated.

"You're not fine, are you?" asked her mother, even though the answer to that was an obvious one.

"I don't mean to complain," said Alice.

"Of course not," agreed her mother.

"But, there is something wrong with this blanket. And the pillowcase," stated Alice.

"And, what is wrong with them?" asked her mother.
"They are too rough," said Alice. "I don't know if you've switched fabric softener, or if I have been sleeping on them for too long, but they are very uncomfortable, and I am not one to complain. "

"Yes, you never complain," agreed her mother. "I thought that something like this may happen, so I have a backup set of sheets and blankets. They are fresh out of the dryer. Would you like to help me put them on?"

"Oh, yes," smiled Alice. "If we change the sheets, pillowcase, and blankets, I am sure that I will sleep soundly.

So, Alice and her mother set to work. They took everything off of the bed, and Alice's mother muttered something about how they should have done this when they were checking the mattress. They replaced the sheet with a new warm, fluffy one, switched the blanket for one that was much softer, and replaced the pillowcase with one that was not so rough.

Alice jumped back into bed and snuggled into the warmth. Alice's mother sat and watched her daughter, waiting for any sign of discomfort.

"You can begin the story, Mother," stated Alice.

One more time, Alice's mother started the story of the elf who had incredibly large ears. "Once upon a time."

Alive kicked the blanket up into the air and let it flutter back down on top of her.

"Once upon a time," said Alice's mother again.

"Whew," whispered Alice.

"Once upon a time." Alice's mother tried to start the story again.

Alice wiped her brow with an exaggerated motion.

"Are you okay?" asked her mother. "Are you not comfortable?"

"No, I am," said Alice. "I mean, the blankets and sheets are comfortable, but they are very warm."

"Warm?" asked her mother.

"Yes, warm," repeated Alice. "They are just out of the dryer and still very warm. Would you mind opening the window a little? But not too much or I will get too cold, and not too little or I will stay warm and be unable to sleep."

Her mother walked to the window, opened it a crack, and let some of the cool breeze trail into the room.

"How is that?" she asked.

"Just right," said Alice.

"So, can we continue with the story?" asked her mother.

"You know," said Alice. "It is getting late, and I am very tired. Maybe we can try to read the story again tomorrow night."

"Yes, tomorrow night," agreed her mother. One of these days they would get past the first line of the story. "Goodnight."

"Goodnight," said Alice. She got herself comfortable and fell fast asleep.

The Elf With Incredibly Large Ears

Once upon a time, there was an elf born with incredibly large ears. When he first appeared, his ears were of average size. Average for an elf, anyway. You see, elf ears are larger than human ears, and they are a little pointed at the top. So, if a human baby was born with elf ears, they would look very big in comparison to human ears. When this elf was born, his ears were the regular size for elf ears.

But, as he grew, his ears did too, and not in a normal elf-ear way. They grew faster than they should and showed no signs of stopping. When he was one-year-old, his ears were the same size as a four-year-old elf's. And, when he was four-years-old, his ears were the same size as an adult elf's. When he turned seven-years-old, his ears were bigger than any other elf's in the village. Even bigger than old-elf-McGonnoggogal, who had the elf record for the biggest ears in the village. (He also had the biggest ears in the elf world, he just did not know it). Well, he *had* the biggest elf ears in the world, all until Bosco turned seven.

When Bosco turned seven, he held the record for having the biggest elf ears that had ever been seen. You would think that this would be something to be proud of, but Bosco was far from proud. In fact, he was a little ashamed of his ears. His large ears brought him a lot of attention, and he did not like that. He wanted to keep to himself and live a simple life, but other elves would not let him.

There were even some who teased him about his ears. Some of the other elves compared him to an elephant, which was not a very accurate comparison. While his ears were large in size, they were not shaped like an elephant's ears. Elephant ears are big and round. While Bosco's ears were big, but they were not round. They stuck straight up in the air and were pointed.

Now, think about your ears. They sit nicely on the side of your head. You are probably happy with the size of them. They are large enough that they don't look weird and small enough so that they don't look extra weird. Now, stick your arms straight up in the air. That is how high Bosco's ears stretched. You can imagine how much of a nuisance that was.

Bosco tried to hide his ears. He would cover his head with large hats, but you need an extra-large hat to cover ears that size. He tried tying them to his head, folding them over, and taping them to the top of his head. That worked for a while, but they would always spring up again. He tried not to go outside, but that was impossible to do. There are so many things to be done outside. Just think of all the things you do outside. There are way too many things to be done to stay inside every day of your life.

"I guess I will just have to accept them," said Bosco.

"Yeah, that's the spirit," shouted Largo. Largo was Bosco's best friend, and he was enthusiastic about everything. Today, they were finally turning sixteen, and that meant they could join the elf army.

The elf army did not do much. They helped other elves build homes, directed traffic when needed, and rescued cats from trees. Yes, there are cats in the elf kingdom. They also wage war with the birds. Every so often, the birds attack, and the elves fend them off.

If you have ever had a bird poop on you, you know how awful that can be. Now, imagine if you have ten thousand birds, and they are all pooping on your village. That is exactly what the elf army faced. When the birds came, they would bang pots and pans together to scare the birds away, but not before the birds had pooped a lot.

Then, the cleanup would begin. You can imagine how awful it is to have to clean bird poop from every house in your entire village, not to mention cleaning up any that fell on the heads of unsuspecting people.

There was one time that they saw the birds coming, but that had been pure luck. No, they just had to deal with it when they arrived.

Bosco and Largo were at the signup for new recruits, and it was not going well for Bosco. While he was the right height and fitness level for the elf army, he could not put on his army hat. His ears were just too big. Finally, they had to cut holes in the hat so that he could wear it.

Next came the obstacle course. That went fine for the most part, but when it came to crawling under the chicken wire, Bosco got his ears caught, and he got stuck. It took three other elves to get him out.

They practiced with paintball guns next. It was a lot of fun to run around and shoot each other with paint, but Bosco was hit more than any other elf. His ears stuck up so much that he could not hide in any bushes or trees. When the day was done, he looked like a rainbow, but he did not feel like one.

"I'm sorry," said the elf general. "I love your enthusiasm, but you are just not cut out to be in the army, Bosco."

"I understand," said Bosco. And, he truly did. His ears had held him back a lot in his life, and this was just another way that they were getting in his way, literally and figuratively.

As he left the elf army compound, he could hear some of the new recruits laughing at him. He was used to that too, and ignored them. As he went home, he knew that he would never be able to help against the bird attacks. He sat in his room and stared out of the window.

"I know that I can help if I am just given a chance," he said to himself.

Bosco sighed and tried to think about what he could do to help, but there was nothing. His ears had gotten in the way again.

With one final push, his ears grew another inch. They had finally reached their full size. No elf had ever had bigger ears, and no elf would.

Bosco sighed again, and a weird sound traveled to him. It sounded like birds. Bosco looked out of the window but could not see any birds. He listened again and was sure that he could hear the squawking of a thousand birds.

He rubbed his ears and knew for sure that the bird squadron was approaching.

Bosco ran as fast as he could to the elf general. He told the general what he had heard. The general believed him immediately. Bosco was not an elf who told lies.

The troops were mobilized. The elf army grabbed their weapons, their pots, pans, and large wooden spoons and began to bang them as loudly as they could.

It was four minutes before the birds appeared.

When the birds got close, the banging noise startled them, and they turned tail and fled. Not one part of the elf village was pooped on that day.

From that day forth, Bosco became the lookout elf, but instead of looking for the birds, he listened for them. Never again was the elf village caught unprepared, and never again were the houses and people covered in bird poop.

The Most Beautiful Places in the World

Have you ever thought about how beautiful the world is?

When you think about it, the world is a marvelous place. There are wonderful things in the world, some that were discovered long ago, some that were discovered recently, and some that have not yet been discovered.

Let's start with an undiscovered place.

Have you ever been swimming, dipped your feet into the ocean, or even just gone underwater in the bathtub? How deep have you swum?

No matter how deep you have gone, you have never gone as deep as the deepest part of the ocean. Do you know how I know that? Because no one has gone there. There are some places in the ocean that have never been seen.

The deeper you go into the ocean, the weirder things start to get. Do you know that there are some sea creatures that live so deep that they are completely blind? There is no light down there, so why would they need to see? There are also fish that can create their own lights, like little flashlights on the top of their heads.

What do you think you would find if you were to dive down to the deepest part of the ocean?

Some people think there are mermaids down there or whole civilizations! I bet there are weird sea creatures down there. Maybe there are starfish with thirty points, or whales bigger than the blue whales, or large dolphins that can talk. What do you think is down there?

Let's move away from the ocean and climb the tallest mountain. Mount Everest is very tall. When you are standing up there, you are as close to the moon as you can get without flying. You can't touch it, though, it's still too far up in the sky.

But, you can look out at the beautiful mountains before you. And, people have been to the top of Mount Everest before, so we know what it looks like up there. The mountain is covered in snow, and that looks very beautiful. The air is also very thin up there, so it is harder to breathe.

I bet there are lots of birds up there. There are lots of clouds too. What shapes do you think they make? Maybe some look like bunnies, and some look like butterflies. Do you think you could see your home from up there? If you were at the top, would you shout something and see how it sounded?

Okay, it's time to come down from there. You cannot live up there. There are no houses, and no food to grow. It's very cold too. I hope that you are tucked up in bed, all nice and warm.

Where shall we go next?

How about on a Safari?

In Africa, there are large patches of land that have lots of cool animals. You could walk through the plains of Africa by yourself, but I wouldn't recommend it. There are lots of wild animals there. Better to fly over in a small plane or drive through in a jeep.

If you spend enough time there, you might see lions and tigers and elephants and meerkats and rhinos and hippos and giraffes and colorful birds. If you could be any of those animals, which one would you be? If you could watch one of those animals, which one would you like to watch?

While we are close, why don't we visit the pyramids!

The pyramids are very cool and were built a long time ago. Some people think that aliens built the pyramids, but it was probably the ancient Egyptians, the people who lived in Egypt. There are still Egyptians in Egypt, but they are not ancient. Some are the same age as you, and some are the same age as your parents or grandparents.

Pyramids are square on the bottom and have triangular sides. Each side meets with the others at a pointy top. They are very big. Think about how big your house is or how big the biggest house is that you have ever seen. The pyramids are a lot bigger.

They also have secret rooms and treasures. If you ever find yourself stuck in a pyramid, don't forget to look for those secret rooms, and you might find some of that treasure.

Where else can you find treasure?

Pirates used to find and hide treasure. They would bury treasure on islands, and draw maps so that they would not forget where they had hidden it. There are no pirates anymore, but there might be some treasure buried on an island somewhere.

Maybe there is some on the island that is far away from everyone. There is one island in the middle of the ocean that is very far away from any people. It is so far away that it is closer to people in space than people on Earth. When the space station passes over, the astronauts inside are closer to the island than any other people on Earth. How cool is that? I bet there is treasure buried there.

Volcanoes can be beautiful too, but don't get to close to them. They are very hot and can erupt at any moment. It is cool to see volcanoes erupt in the ocean. They can't hurt anyone, and sometimes they create new islands. If there were pirates now, I bet that they would hide their treasures on those islands.

What about places where there is no water?

The Sahara desert is like a giant sandpit, except you would have to walk for months to get out of it, if you got lost there. And there is not much water there. But that doesn't stop people from living there. If you know where to look, you can find water. Some is hidden under the ground, and some is hidden inside plants like cactuses.

It is not the best place to live, but it is very beautiful, with sand that stretches as far as the eye can see.

The Antarctic desert is considered the largest desert in the world. This is kind of funny as it is not made from sand but from snow and ice. A desert is a place where it does not rain very much, if at all. That is why the Antarctic is still a desert. It may have lots of snow, but it doesn't rain.

Do you think that you could live there? Snow and ice are very beautiful, but they make it hard to live. You could build an igloo, and that would keep you warm, but food is hard to get, you couldn't just go to the grocery store.

Okay, that is enough of that. I bet that all the talk of snow and ice is making you cold. This is supposed to be a bedtime story that makes you feel all cuddly and warm, not one that makes your toes icy cold.

Let's imagine that your bed is in the desert. As you pull your blanket up over your body, imagine the warm sun beating down on you. If you have a cuddly toy, cuddle up to it. If not, imagine you are cuddling with a stuffed animal, one from the safari.

Wriggle your toes, because that is always fun, and close your eyes. There are so many beautiful places in the world, and you may get to discover one of them when you are older. For now, you can visit them in your dreams.

If there is a place that you would like to visit, imagine that place now. Hold the thought in your mind as you drift off to sleep, and you might just dream about it. If you would like to visit a place in your own imagination, imagine that place in your mind and hold into it as you fall asleep.

Now, lay back, relax, and let your dreams come.

Goodnight.

The Baby Bird Who Fell From Her Nest

There once was a baby bird. This baby bird could not yet fly, but that was okay, for she had a safe nest to live in with her mama and daddy.

One blustery fall day, when Daddy Bird and Mama Bird were out looking for food, Baby Bird was looking out across all of the trees in the forest.

Suddenly, a large gust of wind ripped through the trees and shook the nest. But, Baby Bird did not fall out. She looked out over the trees and smiled as they swayed in the wind.

Another gust came, stronger than the previous one, and shook the tree ferociously. Baby Bird held on with her tiny claws and was glad that she did not fall out.

"I am never going to fall out of this tree," she exclaimed.

Just then, right as she said it, the biggest gust of wind ever felt, passed through the branches. It rustled leaves, ruffled feathers, and rumbled as it moved across the land. You would think that Baby Bird would have been blown from the nest, but she was not.

She laughed at the wind, and did a little dance, flapping her wings. That was when she tripped and fell from the tree.

Down, down, down she went. She flapped her wings, but she could not yet fly. Her talons reached out and gripped a vine. She held onto the vine and swung in a large arc. Through the forest she went until she hit a baby tree. She held onto the tree and slipped down it. Baby Bird hit the ground with a small thump.

Baby Bird squawked. She was well and truly lost. When she looked around, she could not see her mama and daddy, she could not see her nest, and she could not see her tree. She had never left her nest before, and it was a little scary.

"Hello."

Baby Bird turned around in shock. She was not sure what to expect and had definitely not expected to see a tiger standing there. She had read about tigers in books but had never met one before. It looked like a large pussy cat, and she was sure that it was just as tame.

"Are you lost?" asked the tiger.

"Yes," said Baby Bird. "Will you help me to find my tree?"

"Of course," said the tiger, for this was a very helpful and charming tiger. Exactly the kind of tiger that you would invite to tea, if you had a lot of food to be eaten and tea to be drunk.

"Hop on my back." said the tiger. He bent down so that the baby bird could hop up onto his back.

Baby Bird got on and was impressed with how soft the tiger was. As soon as she was on his back, he gave a soft growl and began to walk through the forest.

"Is that your tree?" asked the tiger.

"No, that tree is an oak tree. I live in a silver birch tree. The leaves are the wrong shape," replied Baby Bird.

" How about that tree?" asked the tiger.

"Is the bark silver?" asked Baby Bird.

"No," said the tiger.

"Then that is not the tree," said Baby Bird.

"How about that one?" asked Tiger.

"No," replied Baby Bird.

"That one?"

"Nope."

"That one?"

"No, not that one."

"That one?"

"Definitely not that one."
"How about that one?"

"Look," said Baby Bird. "You need to keep asking me the same question when we pass every single tree."

"But that one has silver bark," said the tiger. "I thought that it might be your silver birch tree."

"Oh, yeah," said Baby Bird, a little embarrassed. "That does look like my tree. Okay, Tiger, up you go."

"What?" asked the startled tiger. "I can't climb trees. I'm a tiger. We are very suited for the ground, thank you very much."

"Well, what am I to do?" asked Baby Bird.

"I can take you."

Baby Bird looked up and saw a monkey hanging in the tree above. He swung back and forth before jumping and doing a somersault through the air, landing on his feet beside the tiger and Baby Bird.

"You really will take me up the tree?" asked Baby Bird.

"Yes, I will," said the monkey with a cheerful smile. "Hop onto my back and hold on tight."

Baby Bird did as she was told. She hopped onto the monkey's back and held on tight to his fur. As soon as she was on, the monkey took off. She did not even have time to say goodbye and thank you to the tiger as they climbed up through the trees.

The monkey was fast and lithe. He gripped a branch, pulled on it, swung on another with his tail, and could reach the next branch up. Baby Bird had expected the monkey to stop at every nest, but he kept going, up and up. Soon it was all a blur to Baby Bird, and she could not make out anything.

But, one thing that she knew for sure was that the nest was at the top of the tree, so she did not say anything to the monkey.

Then, as fast as they had set off, they stopped. Baby Bird looked up and could see her nest only a few meters from where they were.
"That is it," laughed Baby Bird.

"Yes, there is it," said the monkey. "There is only one problem."

"What is it?" asked Baby Bird.

"I cannot go any higher," answered the monkey. "I am much too fast, and the branches are swaying too much. If I go higher, I am afraid that I will fall."

"Well, how am I supposed to get up there?" asked Baby Bird. "I cannot fly, and I cannot climb."

"I…can…help."

Baby Bird looked up and saw a sloth.

"I…can…take…you…up…there," said the sloth very slowly. In fact, Baby Bird almost fell asleep as the sloth talked.

"Oh, thank you," said Baby Bird.

It took the sloth four minutes to get from the branch that he was on to the branch below. When he got there, he scooped up Baby Bird with his long toes and continued the journey upwards. The going was slow, for sloths are very slow creatures.

It took the sloth one minute to pick up Baby Bird, two minutes to introduce himself, and six minutes to plan the route to the top, which was only a few branches away.

They moved so slowly that Baby Bird did fall asleep and would have fallen back to the ground if the sloth was not holding her so tightly.

Baby Bird woke up when the sloth needed to scratch his nose. That took the sloth nine minutes, and then he had to scratch his ear, which took a further eight minutes. From where the monkey had departed to the nest was only two meters, but it took the sloth three hours to get there.

When Baby Bird was safely back in the nest, she did not care. She was home, and she was safe.

"Thank you," said Baby Bird.

"You…are…welcome," said the sloth. That took fifty seconds to say.

The sloth left, and Baby Bird looked out for her mama and daddy to return. It was not long before they did, and Baby Bird danced a dance because she was so happy. As she danced, she tripped and fell from the nest.

Thankfully, Daddy Bird caught her and placed her back in the nest.

"That was close," he said. "You almost fell to the forest floor. You cannot imagine what you would find down there.

Baby Bird hugged her mama and daddy and was happy.

The Unicorn Who Lost His Tail

Many years ago, there lived unicorns. This was back when magic was still alive. There were elves and fairies too, but they are not important to this story, so we are not going to mention them anymore.

There was a short time when unicorns and humans lived together, but that did not last very long before the magical world and the real world separated. This story takes place long before humans were around, and concerns a unicorn by the name of Francisco.

Francisco was a beautiful unicorn. He had grey hair, but not a dirty grey. It was a shiny, clean grey that was luxurious and soft. His mother helped him to brush it every day, and that kept it so soft and lustrous. He also had a silver horn. He was particularly proud of his horn and polished that every day too. It shone like a star.

But, more glorious than his coat and his horn was his tail. Francisco's tail was a rainbow of color. Each strand of hair was a different color and, when it swished, it almost looked like a rainbow shining in the sky.

Francisco loved his tail more than anything in the world, so he was very upset one morning when he woke up and found that his tail was missing. He was sure that he had it the day before, but he could not remember where he had put it.

"Mom! Have you seen my tail?" he shouted.

"Have you checked under the bed?" shouted his mom from downstairs.

"Geez, Mom, of course I have. That was like the first place that I looked," said Francisco.

"Well, keep looking," suggested his mom.

"Obviously," said Francisco. He was a little annoyed at having lost his tail and didn't think that his mom was being helpful.

"But, it is my tail," said Francisco to himself. "I was the one who lost it, so I should be the one to find it."

Francisco tried to think what he had been doing the previous evening, but he had done so much that he did not know where he had left his tail. He decided that he would just have to look everywhere for it.

"I'm going out, Mom. I'm going to go and look for my tail," said Francisco.

"Don't be long," said his mom. "I'm making blueberry pancakes for breakfast.

Francisco loved blueberry pancakes, so he vowed to make the search quick. He ran out of the house, feeling weird without a tail, and searched all over the unicorn kingdom.

The first place he went to was the volatile volcano. He had been there last night, but it was a lot calmer then. He stepped around the edge of the volcano and peered in. As he did, the volcano erupted, and Francisco had to jump back so that his hair was not singed.

Francisco was a very agile unicorn and had amazing balance, but this was a test, even for him. He carefully clip-clopped around the mouth of the volcano. It erupted five more times, and each time he managed to dodge the fiery lava. When he had walked around the mouth of the volcano six times, he decided to search elsewhere. His tail was not in the volcano.

Next up was the dragon cave. Dragons and unicorns are great friends, but not in the early morning. Dragons like to sleep late, and they can be very grumpy if you wake them too early. When Francisco arrived at the dragon cave, the largest and grumpiest dragon was sleeping at its edge.

Fransisco knew better than to wake that particular dragon, so he went into stealth mode. Stealth mode involved standing on the edges of his hooves and stepping extremely lightly.

First, he snuck up to the dragon to make sure that he actually was asleep. Next, he tip-toed past (or tip-hoofed past), heaping an eye on the dragon the entire time. The dragon's chest continued to rise and fall, and small wisps of smoke escaped from its nose.

When Francisco was inside the cave, he was even quieter for any sound would reverberate around the stone cave walls and create even more noise. Francisco searched everywhere that he could think of, but came up empty-handed. The tail was not there.

Next up was the land of the witches. He had been there recently, and his tail could have slipped off.

"Have you seen my tail?" asked Francisco.

"Perhaps," said the oldest witch. "If you can answer me these three riddles, I will tell you where I saw it."

"Okay," said Francisco.

The witch asked the three riddles. Now, these riddles are so difficult that there is no point in recording them here, for they would only succeed in driving your crazy and melting your brain.

Francisco thought long and hard. He had always liked puzzles, but these riddles were extra difficult. He used all of his brainpower, thinking through each one, and he finally came up with three answers.

"Red. The mole was made of ice. Seven-thousand-and-seventy-six," said Francisco.

"Exactly correct," said the witch.

"So, now you will tell me where you saw my tail?" asked Francisco.

"Yes," replied the witch. "I have not seen it anywhere."

Francisco was disappointed. The last place to look was the land of the giants. If his tail was going to be anywhere, then surely it would be there. There was only one problem.

The entrance to the land of giants had been blocked by a landslide. The large arch that usually led to the giant kingdom was blocked by large rocks that had fallen from the mountains above. Francisco set to work.

He moved some of the smaller blocks, using his unicorn strength. He turned the larger blocks and kicked them with his solid hooves, then moved the smaller pieces. It took him a long time, and he started to become hungry, salivating at the thought of the blueberry pancakes that were at home.

When the work was finally done, a large giant approached.

"Hey, thanks for clearing that, I was just coming to do that myself," said the giant.

"Have you seen my tail?" asked Francisco with hope.

"No," said the giant. He walked away.

There was nowhere else to look, and Francisco turned and walked home. If he had a tail, it would have hung low, but he did not have a tail. Instead, he hung his head.

When he got home, the smell of blueberry pancakes was wafting through the house, but he was not in a mood to eat them.

"Did you find it?" asked his mom.

"No," replied Francisco sadly.

"Did you check under your bed?" asked his mom.

"Yes, Mom! I already told you that. Geez, do you think that I am stupid? Look, I'll go and do it again. I've checked under there like three times, but I guess it will magically appear under there if I look again," whined Francisco.

He stomped angrily up the stairs and looked under his bed.

There it was!

That was when he remembered that he had not actually looked under his bed. He smiled to himself, then frowned to himself, then laughed to himself. He wondered if this whole adventure had taught him a lesson.

"Probably not," he murmured.

Francisco went downstairs to find his mom at the kitchen table, serving up pancakes. She glanced at Francisco's magnificent tail but did not say a word. Instead, she served him up some pancakes as he sat down to eat.

Francisco poured some syrup on his pancakes and splashed some on his tail.

Francisco and his mom both laughed.

The Mermaid Who Couldn't Swim

If you have ever read any stories about mermaids, then you know that they are fantastic swimmers. But, mermaids are not born being able to swim, they must learn how to do it, just as you had to learn how to walk.

Now, walking can be tricky, but most people learn how to do it. If you have learned to walk, then well done, and, if not, then you will surely learn how to walk or find another way to get around.

The ocean is a different place, and mermaids cannot get around any other way than swimming. When they are born, they cannot swim, and when they turn three years old, they usually can. Before that age, they are typically strapped to their mothers and carried around or pushed around in large shells.

But, it is widely known that mermaids learn to swim when they are three years old. Well, all except for one.

Aqua was born under a full moon, which is always a sign of good fortune in the underwater world. When she was born, the moonlight was rippling through the water, and a ray of moonshine shone on her head when she first appeared. She looked just like a princess.

But, she didn't act like one. She was very, very, very, very, very, very, very, very stubborn.

She was so stubborn that she did not do anything unless she wanted to do it. That was fine when she was young, but it started to make things a little more difficult when she was older. Especially when she got to three years old.

When she was three, everyone expected her to start swimming. She was stubborn, but that had never held her back. She had always been a mermaid who dreamed big and did everything that she could to achieve her dreams.

Only, it would seem that her dreams did not include swimming.

For the first week after her third birthday, her parents did not think much of it. It was not unusual for some mermaids to start swimming after they were three. The only problem was that Aqua did not even try. She would sit in the sand, not swishing her rich, blue tail, and not going anywhere. And she seemed very pleased with herself.

After a month, her parents started to get worried. Aqua was a healthy young mermaid, but she would not move from her spot in the sand unless she was carried.

"I have an idea," said her mama.

She swam over to Aqua and looked her straight in the eye. "Aqua, I want you to know that I am not going to carry you around anymore. It is time for you to swim by yourself."

"Okay," said Aqua.

Her mama was pleased. When it was time for dinner, her mama called on her and told her that it was time to come home. Aqua said okay, but she did not move. No matter what her mama said, Aqua would not move from her spot. She would not swim.

"Okay, just this one time," said her mama. She picked up Aqua and took her home.

The next day, she was called in for dinner again, Aqua stayed where she was.

" Aren't you going to swim?" asked her mama.

" I'm not ready yet," said Aqua.

"That does not matter," said her mama. "You need to start learning to swim, or you are never going to be able to swim."

This went on for seven more days. Aqua's mama would call her in for food or bath time (yes, mermaids have baths) or bedtime or something else, but Aqua would not swim. Every time, her mama would make an exception and carry her in.

"You are not helping her," said Aqua's father. "Leave this to me, what we need is some tough love."

The family went outside, and Aqua's father told her that they were going to a very special place to play. Aqua asked if she could come, and her father said that she could, all she had to do was to swim with them.
"I don't think that I am ready yet," said Aqua.
"Well, if you don't swim, you won't get to play in this really amazing place," said her father.

"Hmm," mused Aqua. "I do like to play."

"Okay," said her father. "We are going now."

The entire family swam away slowly. They whipped their tails gently, all at the same time, and moved slowly away from Aqua. They pretended to talk about this amazing place they were going to (in actual fact, there was no amazing place. This was all Aqua's father's idea to get Aqua to swim). You can probably guess that it did not work.

The mermaid family hid around the corner and watched. Aqua looked troubled. For a moment, they thought that she was going to swim after them, but she went back to playing in the sand. Aqua's father frowned, but he was not beaten just yet.

He tried again the next day. He told Aqua that they were going for ice cream. There is special ice cream under the water that does not melt like regular ice cream. Aqua loves ice cream, and she was tempted to go with her family, but she was not yet ready to swim.

The next day it was a trip to an underwater volcano, then a weird shark that had a rainbow tail, then a secret cave that may have treasure in it. Aqua was tempted by all of those things, but not tempted enough to do anything about it.

"I know what to do," said Willow, Aqua's sister. "She just needs to see us swimming around her more."

Aqua's parents did not know what to do, and this was their last option, so they agreed.

Willow, and Aqua's two other sisters, swam as much as they could around Aqua.

"Look at us," said Willow. "Look at what we can do. Isn't this cool!"

"Yeah, it's pretty cool," said Aqua.

"Don't you want to join us?" asked Willow.
"When I am ready," said Aqua.

Willow and her sisters swam fast in a line, darting past Aqua trailing a long line of bubbles behind them. They found some dolphins and rode on their backs. They swam in large circles, looping upside down, then around and around. They placed various loops and tunnels and swam through them as fast as they could. They even got a blue whale to agree to help them, and the sisters swam in and out of its mouth.

"Doesn't this look fun?" asked Willow.

"So much fun," agreed Aqua.

Still, she did not swim. Willow and her sisters tried this for an entire month, but Aqua did not move from her spot in the sand.

Six months after her third birthday, Aqua's parents gave up. "I don't think that she is ever going to swim," said her mother.

"Hey, would you look at that," said her father.

They looked outside to see Aqua swimming. Not only that, but she was the most magnificent swimmer that they had ever seen. She streaked past, swimming faster than any other mermaid could. She corkscrewed and twisted. She beat her tail, creating gigantic bubbles. She even swam to the surface, jumped out, did three backflips, and landed gracefully back in the water.

When Aqua swam home, her parents stared at her in disbelief. Their mouths hung open wide, not able to believe what they were seeing. Aqua had not swum for six months, and now she was the best swimmer in the ocean.

Aqua stopped in front of her house and looked at her disbelieving parents. "I guess that I was ready," she said. She swam away to play with her sisters, go to an exciting place, and find some ice cream or treasure.

The Four Little Pigs

Everyone knows the story of the three little pigs, but not many people know the story of the four little pigs, for those three brothers had a sister who ran away to join the circus, and that story is quite amazing. Can you believe that a pig could join the circus? Well, this story is about how all four pigs eventually joined the circus, and the wolf was never really to blame.

Now, in the traditional story, the three little pigs are scared of the wolf, for no reason other than he is not a pig, and they lose their houses. Let's start a little before that.

When the four little pigs first came to Wolfsville, they thought that it was a great place to start a new life. All except for the youngest pig, Geraldina. She did not want to live in a city, and she had tried to convince her brothers to join the circus with her.

The three brothers were afraid of height, did not like clowns, and were terrified of doing anything in front of a crowd.

"This is the life for me," said Abe, the oldest pig.

"Yes, I will be quite safe here," agreed Gabe, the middle brother.

"Oh, yes, a nice city life with a boring job," chimed Babe, the youngest of the three brothers.

So, the three little pigs set up a new life in the city of Wolfsville. Abe found a job as an accountant, Gabe found a job as an accountant, and Babe found a job as an accountant. And, they were all happy, for precisely seven minutes.

Meanwhile, Geraldina joined the circus and did boring circus things like put her head in a lion's mouth, walk the tightrope that was three miles high, juggle nine balls of fire, and clean up the elephant dung. She was happy for precisely seven minutes, and then she was happy for every single minute after that.

But, Geraldina missed one thing. Well, she missed three things. She missed her three older brothers. She sent regular postcards detailing precisely what she had been up to, and she enjoyed hearing from her brothers, even if they talked a lot about accounting.

Back in the city of Wolfsville, the three brothers were starting to grow tired of their jobs. The first seven minutes had been a lot of fun, but they were starting to get tired of numbers. But, the three pig brothers were not ones to give up, so they decided to start building homes. They did not have enough money to stay in a hotel for their entire lives.

This is partly where the original fairytale starts. As you may have guessed, Babe made a home out of straw, Gabe made a home out of sticks, and Abe made a home out of bricks. You are probably thinking that bricks are a suitable material for a home, but why would you build a home out of straw and sticks?

You may be thinking that the pigs did not want their homes to last for a long time, and you would be right. Gabe and Babe were already thinking about moving away from Wolfsville and joining the circus with their sister, but they were a little scared to make that leap.

"Maybe our houses will fall down," suggested Gabe.

"Then we can join the circus," said Babe.

There had been many postcards from their sister, and they were longing for a life without numbers, and with more elephant poo.

There was only one problem. While their houses were made from straw and sticks, they were still well built. They did not want to destroy their own houses, for they were still not sure about joining the circus. They were hoping that something would make the decision for them, and they would have no choice. Pigs can be funny like that.

Thankfully for Gabe and Babe, something did come along. Rather, *someone* came along. Wilfred, the wolf, was a building inspector, and he was in charge of all of the buildings in Wolfsville. After the three new houses were built by the pig brothers, he scheduled a time to come and visit them.

Wilfred was a very nice wolf and was known all around the community as the nice, little wolf. It is astounding, then, that his name was eventually changed to the big, bad wolf. He was never big, and he was never bad.

When he got to Babe's house, he was amazed.

"How can you live in a house of straw?" asked Wilfred.

"I don't know," said Babe.

"This house is going to come down when the first breeze hits it," said Wilfred. To illustrate this, he blew on the house, and the entire house collapsed.

Babe pretended to be sad, but he was secretly happy. He could finally join the circus. He skipped after the wolf as Wilfred went to visit Abe.

When Wilfred got to Abe's house, he was astounded.

"Why would you ever build a house from sticks?" asked Wilfred.

"I don't know," said Gabe.

"You have not even used any glue or tape," said Wilfred. "The first time that an earthquake hits, this house is going to come crumbling down. It is a health hazard."

"I don't know what I was thinking," said Gabe.

To illustrate what an earthquake would be like, Wilfred shook the house gently. The entire house of sticks came tumbling down.

"I'm sorry," said Wilfred.

"That's okay," said Gabe. Secretly, he was happy. He could finally run away and join the circus.

Gabe and Babe followed Wilfred as he went to visit Abe. When Wilfred got to Abe's house, he was pleasantly surprised. He found a well-built house, made of bricks.

"This is a very fine house," said Wilfred. "It will survive wind, earthquakes, and pretty much anything else that you can throw at it."

"Thank you," said Abe. He felt proud but sad at the same time. He wanted to join the circus too, but he was also a sensible builder of houses.

When Wilfred left, the three pig brothers were left alone.

"You can live here with me if you like," said Abe.

"No, we are going to run away and join the circus," said Gabe.

"Yeah, we are done being accountants. We are going to be clowns or trapeze artists or jugglers," said Babe.

"Well, then let's get to work," said Abe. "I can't leave if I have a perfectly good house to live in."

The three brothers set about demolishing the brick house. They used hammers and chisels to remove the bricks. They smashed everything inside, ripped up everything on the outside, and made a really big mess.

When Wilfred returned (he had forgotten his hat), he found a pile of bricks with a hat on the top. He shook his head and was glad that the three funny pigs had left. They were nice pigs, but they were not very good at building houses.

The three little pigs started a new life. They packed what little they had, found the traveling circus, and joined Geraldina. They became the most astounding pigs that had ever been seen. The four of them became expert jugglers, they all walked the high wire at the same time, and they flew through the air as trapeze artists.

The finale of every show involved them each placing their heads inside of a lion's mouth. The crowd would always go wild, and that made the pigs happy. They had been bored as accountants, and they had finally found something that they loved doing.

Of course, they still took care of the circus accounts; they were trained to deal with numbers, after all.

The Princess and the Prince

There once was a handsome prince. He lived in the wealthiest kingdom in all the land. He was tall, had long, flowing golden hair, dressed in the most stylish clothes, wore shiny shoes, treated everyone very kindly, had lots of friends, was very mature for his age, worked hard, had a pet iguana, and longed to find a wife.

He would walk about all day and say things like, "Nice job!" and "You look good today!" and "What a nice person you are!" and "Have some of my ice cream!"

Everybody loved the prince, and the prince loved everybody.

On the other side of the kingdom, there lived a princess. She had long, straggly locks of hair that she never brushed, she liked to wear the same clothes every day, she was kind but shy, had a pet dog (that was very scruffy), often got angry at the injustice in the world, but always wore a smile on her face.

While she could come across as brash, everyone in the castle loved her, because she had a true heart and would always speak the truth, though that sometimes hurt people a little.

She would say things like, "You need to help out more," or "Why are you wearing so many rings?" or "Stop worrying about what people think of you and have some fun," or "I like ice cream."

There is one more character in this story: the big dragon who lives in the mountains. Dragons like to steal helpless people, and I bet that you can guess what happened next. Yes, the dragon flew to the kingdom, swooped down into the gardens, and stole the handsome prince.

Well, the kingdom was in an uproar. That prince had been due to marry a beautiful princess from another kingdom, and the king and queen were very upset.

"I am upset," said the king.

"I am very upset," said the queen.

They decided to do all that they could to save the prince. They assembled all of the soldiers that they had, armed them with the very best weapons, and sent them off to rescue the prince. They returned a few days later with very burnt clothes. When the princess heard that her betrothed had been captured by a dragon, she was extremely upset.

"I am extremely upset," said the princess.

"I am upset, too," said her father.

"Yes, me too," said her mother.

They decided that if the king and queen of the other kingdom could not save the prince, they would have to do it instead. They were a king and queen too, and they had an army also. They called in all their best knights, equipped them with the very best armor, and sent them to save the prince.

The knights returned a few days later with extremely burned armor, and no prince. They gave up, for there was absolutely nothing that they could do. The prince was lost forever.

Meanwhile, Princess Anastasia, the one with the straggly hair, was brooding in her room. She had not been allowed to climb on the castle roof as it was far too dangerous. Well, she would just have to think of something else.

"Father, why can't I play on the roof?" she asked the next day.

"It is much too dangerous," said her father, who was also a king. There once was a lot of kings and queens in the world.

"Well, I suppose that I will have to find something safer to do," said Anastasia.

"Yes, I suppose that you will," agreed the king.

"Perhaps I will go and fight the dragon so that the prince can be free," suggested Anastasia.

"Yes," agreed her father. "That sounds like a nice way to spend your day, and not at all dangerous."

So, Princess Anastasia gathered some of her belongings, her best leather armor, a sharp steel sword, a large wooden shield, and some food. She left the castle on a horse, munching on an apple as she rode.

It was a long way to the mountains, and there were some obstacles to overcome first. In the wetlands, she had to dismount her horse and lead it through the shallower waters. When they were out the other side, she got back on the horse and rode again.

"Well done, Hamish," said Anastasia. Hamish was the name of her horse.

The jungle was next. Anastasia dismounted again and used her sword to hack her way through large branches and vines. Some of the vines even reached out to grab her, but she was much too quick. There were large spiders too, but they were friendly, and one even came along for the ride.

The quicksand was next. At the edge of the quicksand, there was a sign:

Enter ye, all who dare!
But of the sand, beware, beware!
Once you enter, you don't get out!
No matter if you scream or shout!

Anastasia looked out across the quicksand and thought about what to do. It would be dangerous to go through the quicksand, and she did not want to get stuck. So, she decided to go around. It was not too much out of her way, and it only added three more minutes to her journey.

The swampland was next, and she had to go through that, for there was no other way to get to the mountain. She tread very carefully, guiding Hamish so that he did not get sucked into the swampy mud. At one point, a large swamp monster appeared, but they are deathly afraid of spiders, so it quickly ran away.

After the swamp, they reached the mountains. It was tough going, constantly ascending the steep, craggy rock, but Hamish was an excellent horse, and Anastasia was an excellent rider. When they reached the mouth of the cave, Anastasia dismounted and shouted:

"DRAGON! GET OUR HERE, I NEED TO HAVE A WORD WITH YOU!"

The dragon was there in seconds. Anastasia can shout very loud, and the dragon looked scared when he came out of the cave, but quickly regained his composure when he saw that a princess was standing there.

"Let the prince go!" demanded Anastasia.

"No," said the dragon.

"I thought that you would say that," said Anastasia. "So, I have come prepared to fight. Will you face me?"

"Yes," said the dragon.

The fight began.

The dragon leaped into the air, flapping its large wings, almost pinning Anastasia to the ground. A plume of fire came next, shooting from the dragon's mouth, straight at Anastasia. She managed to roll and dodge the first blast, but the second came all too soon. She blocked it with her shield and could feel the searing heat.

Quickly, she rolled behind a rock and out of sight. She clambered up the cave entrance and positioned herself behind the dragon. While the great beast searched for her, she leaped onto its back and ran up its spine. When she reached the dragon's head, she did a somersault, leaped up into the air, came back down, and bonked the dragon on the nose with her sword.

Tears welled in the dragon's eyes, and it quickly flew away. When the dust had settled, the handsome prince emerged from the cave. He was a little dirty but still looked extremely dashing in his regal clothes.

"Thank you for saving me," said the prince. "I was due to marry another princess, but I will now marry you for being so brave."

"No thank you," said Anastasia. "I have many more adventures to go on, and I cannot yet think about marrying someone. I am much too young."

"Oh," said the prince.

They both went home to their kingdoms, and the prince married the princess that he had been promised to.

Anastasia continued to have adventures until she was ninety-nine. She fought many more dragons, found endless treasure, and even brought peace to the entire kingdom.

The Trees Throw a Party

There are some people who ask the classic question: if a tree falls in the forest, and no one is around to hear it, does it make a sound?

What they should be using is what music do trees like to dance to?

Trees don't often just fall over for no reason, but they do like to dance and do it quite often. When all of the people have cleared out of the forest, and no one is close by to see them, the trees often throw a party.

At this party, there is lots of singing and dancing. Most trees are horrible singers, and you never want to hear a tree sing, but they are the most amazing dancers and, if you ever get to see them dance, you will agree with all your heart.

Once a year, when the Northern Lights are the brightest, the trees throw the biggest party. The animals will often come to visit and watch the trees dance, and if you are a friend of the trees, you might be invited too.

Not many people have seen trees dancing.

The oak trees are always the ones to get the party started. During the day, they stand magnificently in the forest, regal and mighty. They hold acorns in their hands, gifting some to the squirrels for food, and dropping others to the ground to grow more oak trees.

As soon as the Northern Lights are shining, the oak trees start to dance. Their dances are a simple one. They sway from side to side as if they are moving with the wind, but there is no wind, they are dancing. The more they sway, the higher they lift their branches, as if they are trying to touch the stars.

This signifies the start of the dancing party, and all of the other trees join in. The weeping willows are usually next.

Weeping willows have long branches that hang down to the ground. Imagine someone who is crying, with their head and hands hanging down. This is how the weeping willow looks, only as a tree. While weeping willows look sad, they are one of the happiest trees at the party.

When they start to feel the Northern Lights 'music, they bop side to side, as if they are dancing with their shoulders. Of course, trees do not have shoulders, but the dance looks like this.

When they dance, they smile wide and laugh. If you were another tree, you would spot this immediately. If you look closely, you might see it. Their leaves start to quiver, and this is them smiling. Then leaves also make a rustling noise, and this is their laughter. The weeping willows, and the oak trees dance together in time.

The silver birch trees come next, though they have to be careful as birds often nest in their trees. These trees like to breakdance. While the weeping willows and oaks are moving side to side, the silver birch trees move their branches like they are robots.

Some of them, the more experienced dancers, will crouch down and throw their roots out to one side and then the other. If you are lucky, you may see them spin on the forest floor, sometimes on their heads.

The weeping willows always receive massive cheers from the other trees, and this gets the party started, with all of the other trees joining in.

The palm trees are the jokers of the tree worlds. They like to take their own coconuts and bang them together in time with the music of the Northern Lights. They slowly beat their coconuts faster and faster, causing every tree to dance quicker and quicker until their branches cannot keep up, and the trees fall to the floor.

The palm trees laugh but soon help everyone up, and they each find a partner to dance with. They love the old ballroom dances, and will often waltz around the forest with the other trees. If you were to look down on the trees from above, like the Northern Lights can, you would see all of the trees moving together, each with a partner, and each moving in and out of the other.

It is a beautiful thing to see, and the palm trees are amazing dancers, even if they do like to cause mischief.

The baby trees join in next. Once they have seen the adult trees dancing, they want to join in and do the same. They imitate the older trees and hone their dancing skills so that they will be expert dancers when they are older.

Next, come all of the fruit trees from the orchards. None of these trees dance like any other, and they all freestyle dance, doing their own thing, but still following the music. As the other trees are dancing together, the fruit trees weave in and out, and dance in time with those around, but performing dance moves that no other can. This helps to make their fruit even sweeter and delicious for when you get your hands on it.

The sycamore and pine trees like to dance together. When they arrive at the party, they select a partner and dance with that partner for the entire night. They often split into groups of eight, and perform dances together, dancing in jigs or reels, switching partners, but always ending back with their original partner.

It is fun to watch a tree spin back and forth between dance partners, and the sound of the swishing leaves when this happens is unlike anything else that you can imagine.

As the trees dance under the Northern Lights, the colors become rich and vivid. There are greens, blues, purples, reds, and yellows in the sky, colors dancing to their own tune. Down below, the leaves all start as green but soon change to every color of the rainbow.

The greens are too many to count, and, as the trees dance, their leaves change color as if every season is happening at once. Greens become yellows, oranges, reds, browns, blacks, whites, and then green again. The leaves look like an ocean as they all dance together.

More and more trees come from all around, all of them dancing their own dance, and smiling and laughing. This is the most joyous occasion for the trees.

The giant sequoia trees always arrive last. They are so big that it takes them longer than any other tree to get there. They tower above the forest, with thick red trunks that seem to stretch up to the sky. When they come, they start to sing in low booming voices, making the ground tremble. It sounds like a thousand musicians playing tubas, trumpets, and drums, all at the same time.

The trees all come together and sway from side to side in time with the choir of sequoia trees. If you were there, you would feel the entire forest shaking, and you would not be able to stop swaying with the trees.

When the song is done, the trees all leave and return home. As the sun rises, the Northern Lights leave to sleep. The forest returns to normal.

So, the next time you find yourself in a forest and you feel like dancing, please do. The trees love to see people dance and, if you don't tell anyone, they might just dance with you too.

The Nice Dragon

Detrimus is a very common name for a dragon. Meteor is also very popular, and Flame is a not-so-original name that has been passed down through the generations. You will find many Flame Juniors and Flame the thirds. It was confusing then, that Edgar was called Edgar, and he often puzzled over his name.

"Why did you call me, Edgar?" Edgar asked when he was five.

"It suited you," said his mother. "When you were born, you looked like an Edgar."

Edgar had to agree. When he looked at himself in the mirror, he did not look like a Brodgar or a Fireball or even a Smoky. He looked just like an Edgar, so he learned to love his name.

As he lay in bed that night, he forgot all about his name and worried more about starting school. Tomorrow was going to be his first day at dragon school, and he was a little bit nervous about it. He had some friends starting with him (Flame, Flame Jr, and Destroyer), but that did not help to calm his nerves.

When he woke up the next morning, Edgar dressed in his new dragon school uniform, ate his charred pancakes, and walked to school. Thankfully, it was not far. When he got there, he found his friends, and they all went to class together.

The classes were pretty simple, and he was taught English and Math. Even though dragons don't need to write, they do need to read. They need to make sure that the treasure they find is not fake. They also need to read signs so that they know where they are going when they are stealing princesses.

After lunch, how to steal princesses was the next class. They learned how to swoop down, grab a princess, and then hide her in a cave. They practiced outside with watermelons and hid them in trees.

"Why do we steal princesses?" asked Edgar.

"Because they are princesses," said his teacher as if that was an acceptable answer.

"Yes, but why?" asked Edgar.

"Because we have always done it," said his teacher.

"But, why did we start?" asked Edgar.

"Because we are dragons," replied his teacher, giving a smile as if he had just solved a complicated problem.

This did not satisfy Edgar, and the questioning continued for a long time after this until the school bell rang, and it was time to move onto the next class. Edger did not get an answer that he liked.

"Stop being a troublemaker," said one of his classmates, a large red dragon with sharp teeth.

"I'm just trying to be nice," said Edgar.

"Well, dragons are not nice," replied the red dragon.

"Why not?" asked Edgar.

"Because we are dragons," said his classmate. The red dragon walked off as if he had given a satisfactory answer. He had not. Not for Edgar, anyway.

The next class was all about how to find treasure and how to store it. Edgar had to admit that this class was fun. It was like hide and seek but, instead of other dragons hiding, there was gold hidden. The dragons had to search for it, like a treasure hunt or a scavenger hunt.

When all the gold had been found, the dragons stood around it. The large pie of gold was impressive and shiny.

"Why do we hoard treasure?" asked Edgar.

"What kind of a stupid question is that?" asked his teacher. "What else are you supposed to do with treasure?"

"But, we can't spend it or use it," said Edgar.

"No," said the teacher, waiting for Edgar to get to the point.

"Then, why do we hoard it?" asked Edgar again.

"Because it is treasure," said the teacher. He folded his arms as if he had answered all of Edgar's questions, and the young dragon would now thank him for being so wise.

"What if we didn't hoard treasure?" asked Edgar. "What if we did something else. Hoarding treasure is so time consuming and dangerous."

"If we didn't hoard treasure, then we would have no treasure," said the teacher.

"Exactly," said Edgar.

"Exactly," responded his teacher as if they were in agreement.

They were not. Nothing that his teachers said made any sense to Edgar, and they were supposed to be his teachers. What chance did he have in life if he was not going to be able to get answers to any of his questions?

The final class of the day was about fighting knights. The life of a dragon is hazardous, and they are under constant attack by knights.

The dragons learned how to dodge arrows, sidestep swords, and duck under maces. They also learned how to hurl fire and practiced on straw dummies. Edgar had a lot of fun doing this, but he did have some questions.

"Why do knights attack us?" asked Edgar.

"Because we steal treasure and princesses," replied his teacher as if this was the most obvious thing in the world.

"What if we didn't steal that stuff?" asked Edgar. "Isn't stealing bad?"

"Then we wouldn't have that stuff," said the teacher. "Without stealing that stuff, we wouldn't be able to fight so many knights."

"Wouldn't that make it safer to be a dragon?" asked Edgar. "If we didn't steal things that we didn't need, then we wouldn't have to fight knights that we don't have to fight."

"Ah, you are still young," said the teacher. He lowered his voice so that he could whisper. Sometimes adult dragons like to whisper to make what they say seem more important. "It is dragon nature to steal treasure and princesses. That is just who we are. Just as knights like us to steal that stuff as it is in their nature to fight dragons. If we didn't steal, they would have nothing to do. If we didn't steal stuff, we wouldn't have anything to do, and then where would we all be? It's very complicated. I wouldn't expect a young dragon like you to understand."

Edgar didn't understand it, but it didn't seem complicated. It seemed very simple.

The teacher ushered the students away with a big smile on his face as if he had just solved all of their problems.

Edgar stopped asking questions. While the teachers had a lot of answers, they never really answered what he was asking. He decided to take a different approach. As he grew up, he didn't steal anything and was nice to everyone instead. It took a lot of work for the humans to trust him, but eventually, they did.

Instead of stealing princesses and treasure and fighting knights, Edgar used his skills to move large rocks or fuel furnaces. The world's humans appreciated his hard work and knew that he was different from the other dragons.

They would pay him in food and other useful things, but Edgar still accepted some treasure, as he knew that the older dragons liked that sort of thing. It was very shiny but completely useless.

When the other dragons saw him bring the useful items and useless treasures home, they marveled at how he had collected so much. When he told them that the humans had just given them to him, they did not believe him at first.

The younger dragons joined him on some of his excursions, and they found that they could earn whatever they desired by doing a little work. It was certainly easier than sealing, definitely more fun, and there was a limited threat from knights.

As more and more dragons took up this new life, more and more joined in. Soon, all of the dragons had given up their old life of stealing and were soon working with the humans to help them, and help themselves.

"I knew that I gave you the right name," said Edgar's mother one night as they were sat at home. "You are not a Destroyer, or a Flame, or a Smoky. You are definitely an Edgar."

Edgar could not help but agree.

The Wrong Potion

Agnes was not born with the name Agnes, but when she became a witch, she renamed herself. When she was born, her name had been Petunia Sunflower Witherington. When she became a witch, at the age of sixteen, she renamed herself Agnes Broomstick.

Of course, she did not tell her family that she had become a witch. They would not believe her if she did tell them, so it was best to keep that kind of thing to herself.

Agnes moved to a small wooden shack in the woods, a classic destination for most witches, and told her family that she had moved to the big city to work as a secretary. They were happy that she had a job, and Agnes was happy that she would never have to work in a boring job. Witches have ways of making money, from selling potions to those who believed in witches, to curing ailments that cannot be cured by doctors, to turning bad people into frogs.

Agnes specialized in making potions. In fact, she was one of the best witches around at making potions, even though they sometimes went very wrong.

The potions that she would make could turn people into any animal they wanted, could give you superpowers, and could help your tomato plants to grow more tomatoes.

She had just received an order from a man who needed the boils removed from his face.

"Easy, easy, easy," said Agnes when the man contacted her. "Removing boils is one of the easiest potions in the world."

"Oh, good," said the man. "He had called Agnes from his office and needed the boils to be gone by lunchtime. He had a very important meeting to go to after lunch, where he and his business associates would talk about very boring things that they were very interested in.

"Yes, I will deliver it myself," said Agnes. "Just tell me one thing, how many boils do you have? It is very important to know the exact number so that I can add the exact ingredients."

"I have thirteen boils," said the man.
"AAAAAAAAAAYYYYYYYYEEEEEEEIIIIIIIIII!!!!!!!!!" screamed Agnes.

The businessman almost dropped the phone, the scream had been so loud.

"Sorry," said Agnes when she had regained her composure. "Boils are easy, but not so much when you have thirteen of them. That is the worst number of boils that you can have."

"Can you help me?" asked the businessman. There was a lot of worry in his voice, and he was starting to suspect that he would have to skip his important meeting. He held the phone to his ear and waited. It felt like an eternity before Agnes Broomstick spoke again.

"Yes, I can do it," she said.

"Thank you," said the businessman. He hung up the phone and checked himself one more time in the mirror. His face was covered in thirteen big, green boils.

Agnes hung up the phone on her end. She did not have a phone, but she did have a log that she spoke into, so she placed the log back down in its holder.

"This is going to be harder than I thought," said Agnes. "If he had twelve boils, I could whip up a potion in sixty seconds, and if he had fourteen boils, I could have a potion ready in half that time. Thirteen is an unlucky number, and this is going to take some time, but I am sure that I can get it done by lunchtime."

Agnes Broomstick liked a challenge, and this was certainly going to be a challenge. She pulled out her extra-large cauldron from the cupboard and placed it in the middle of her room, directly over the small woodpile. She lit a fire beneath it and got to work.

First, came all of the regular ingredients that make up most witch potions. She added thirteen spider legs, thirteen eyes of newt, thirteen pinches of salt, and thirteen bat wings. As she stirred the potion in large circles, she felt satisfied that the potion making was going well.

"I think that this is going to go without a hitch," said Agnes. "I do not think that there are going to be any problems whatsoever."

Next, came the crucial part. There were two ways that she could go with this potion. She could add the blue food coloring to give the potion a nice blue tint, or the red food coloring to give the potion a nice red tint.
One color would create the correct potion, and the other could end the world. She always got the two mixed up, but was sure that the blue food coloring was the right one. She dumped the entire bottle into the potion and took a step back. When nothing happened, she breathed a sigh of relief.

"Right, as always," she whispered.

She continued on with the potion. She added some lemongrass, one cat hair, some globulous goo, ten sprigs of heather, and a willow wisp. That is when the trouble began. As she added the willow wisp, the potion started to bubble ferociously and let out a large gargled burp. The burp covered Agnes and turned her skin completely green.

This put Agnes in a panic. She was now sure that she had put in the wrong color. She would have to do everything in her power to save the potion. She threw in tree bark, and the potion almost exploded. A dark cloud appeared over her small shack. When it started to rain, it rained cats and dogs. Cats and dogs began dropping from the sky with lots of meows and barks.

To combat this, she added some oregano. That only succeeded in growing the cloud, and it soon covered the entire world, raining cats and doge over the entire planet.

When Agnes added some cocoa powder and essence of frog, everything started to shrink, and I mean everything. Her cauldron, her home, her forest, her country, and the entire planet started to shrink. It would only be a few minutes before it shrank into nothing.

She threw in seven rat tails, which caused everyone in the world to turn into jelly. That would be a problem, but at least the businessman would not have to go to his meeting. When she threw in red berries, all of the water in the world turned into hot chocolate. She added sugar to the cauldron, but that did not help.

Pickles and paprika were added next, and that turned the world inside out. It was still raining cats and dogs, people were made from jelly, all the water was hot chocolate, and the world had turned inside out.

Right before the world disappeared from existence, Agnes threw her watch into the cauldron and stirred it in the opposite direction. Everything reversed, and she was taken back in time. All the cats and dogs were sucked back up into the sky, the world grew back to normal size, people were not jelly anymore, and the water was water again.

Agnes found herself holding the blue and red food coloring bottles, wondering which one to add.

"I guess I should add the red one this time," she said. She dumped in the red food coloring, took a step back, and was happy when it turned a nice pink color. She added the rest of the ingredients and ladled the mixture into a bottle.

It was 11.30 am when she hopped onto her broomstick with the boil-removal potion. She flew quickly to the offices of the businessman and delivered the potion. He quickly uncorked the bottle, drank it all, and licked his lips. As soon as he had drunk it, the boils vanished from his face.

Agnes was glad that he could go to his meeting.

She was also glad that she had not destroyed the entire world.

The Bee Who Loved All of the Flowers

Bees love flowers more than any other creature in the world, even curious little boys and girls, but there is one bee that loves flowers more than anyone else.

Bert is a busy bee. He loves to fly from flower to flower and collect pollen. That pollen is one of the things he loves about flowers. Bert loves that the pollen us turned into honey and that he can share all of that honey with people around the world.

It is a magical transition, and Bert still marvels when it happens. The bright yellow pollen that he collects is turned into yummy honey for people to enjoy.

But that is not the main reason why he loves flowers so much.

He loves flowers so much because every flower is different and every flower is beautiful. Even though some flowers are the same variety, they always have slightly different colors, or the petals are shaped differently; some are short while others are tall, and they even smell different.

Some flowers don't hold the pollen that Bert needs, but he still likes to visit them. He always makes sure to visit all of the flowers so that none of them feel left out. Flowers have feelings too.

The sunflowers are his absolute favorites, and they are always the flower that he visits first. There is a bonus reason as to why he visits this flower first and that it down to their size.

When Bert first wakes up in the morning, much like any bumblebee, he is very tired. I am sure it is the same if you have to wake up early.

When he is still sleepy, it is hard to stay focused when he is flying. That makes sunflowers perfect. They are so tall and big that they are easy to see when it is still early in the morning, and the sun is not yet fully up.

Sunflowers look like mini suns, making them the perfect flower for Bert to visit. They are so easy to see that it is the perfect start to his day. Of course, they are beautiful and magnificent too.

"Good morning, sunflowers," Bert says as he arrives at the sunflowers and hovers in front of them for a while.

Once he has visited them, he plays feels more awake.

Next, Bert visits the orchids. They are a delicate flower, and they come in all the colors of the rainbow. While Bert does not play favorites with the flowers, he would admit that orchids are the most beautiful.

One thing that he likes about visiting orchids in the early morning is that they always match a color that is in the sky. As the sun starts to rise, the sky goes through many different colors, starting as black, becoming more purple, before moving through red, orange, yellow, green, and blue.

As Bert visits the orchids, he can find an orchid to match every color of the sky, and that is a good way to wakeup. As he flies from flower to flower, it gives him his morning exercise, which helps wake him up and get ready for his day.

"Good morning, orchids," Bert says.

Once Bert is ready to start the hard work, he goes straight for the flowers that give the most pollen. The next stop is always lavender. Not only is lavender a great producer of pollen, and perfect for making honey, but it also smells amazing. If you have ever passed under a lavender bush and breathed in deeply, then you will know exactly what I mean.

"Good morning, lavender," Bert says when he arrives at the flower.

Now, he gets to work. He collects as much pollen as he can before he starts to feel sleepy. It is a lot of work to collect pollen. When he has collected enough, it is time to think about a morning nap.

Poppies and tulips are perfect for sleeping in. Bert's favorite color has always been red, and he loves to nap in red petals. Poppies and tulips are very soft too, and perfect for a bee to take a nap in. The flower he chooses will depend on which he is closest to.

"Good morning, tulips," he will say if he chooses tulips and, "Good morning, poppies," he will say if he chooses poppies. "May I sleep in you."

The flowers will always agree because they love to have bees sleeping in them. Bert likes to sleep for forty-five minutes, and he always feels very energized after that. When he wakes up, he goes off in search of bluebells.

Bluebells look like mini street lamps but, instead of having white or yellow lamps on the top of long poles, they have droopy, blue lamps. Bert always feels very sneaky when he has to go underneath the flower and fly up into it. He feels like a bee ninja who is stealing the pollen, though he never actually steals it, the flowers want him to have it.

"Good afternoon, bluebells," Bert says.

When he is done with the bluebells, it is time to have a little fun. It is time to visit the dandelions.

First, he lands on the bright yellow dandelions and dances around on the top of the flower. They are so soft, and it is like being on a really thick carpet. After that, he finds the dandelion with the fluffs on the top. He flies past them as fast as he can, beating his wings, and trying to lift as much of the fluff as possible to see it flying through the air.

"Good afternoon, dandelions," Bert says as he flies past.

After he has had his fun, Bert flies off in search of crocuses. Crocuses are big, bold, bright flowers with lots of pollen. Crocus is a fun word to say too, and Bert likes to say it over and over in his head as he flies towards them.

" Good afternoon, crocuses, crocuses, crocuses," Bert says.

He does not have much room left by this point, so he collects as much as he can carry, and his pollen collecting is done for the day. But, there is still time to visit a few more flowers before he goes home.

"Good Afternoon, daisies," Bert says as he flies past them. He loves the large white petals and yellow center. It reminds him of the eggs that he once saw in a house he was trapped in. Thankfully the owner opened the window and let him out.

Good evening, hibiscus," Bert says as the sun starts to go back down. All the colors of the rainbow will soon be seen in the sky again, and that will mean that it is time for him to be in the hive. He likes the smell of hibiscus and knows that some humans make tea from it. Bert hopes that they add some of his honey to that tea.

"Good evening, magnolias," Bert says when he gets to the large white flowers. After seeing so much color throughout the day, it is nice to see a plain white flower, and Bert finds a lot of beauty there.

"Good evening, lotus," Bert says. This is his last stop of the evening. They have perfectly shaped petals, and they always seem to sway in the wind as he passes, like they are waving to him.

As Bert flies back to the hive, he is sad that he cannot visit more flowers. They are all so beautiful that he wishes he could stay out and visit more, but it is getting late, and he needs to deliver his pollen. Bert is getting tired, too, even with his morning nap.

When he gets home, he delivers his pollen and finds his bed. When he falls asleep, he dreams only of flowers. Bert cannot wait to wake up and visit the flowers again.

Uncle Ron Babysits

Hello.

My name is Albert, and I am a dinosaur. Most people call me Alby, and you can, too, if you want. You are reading this story about me, so you might as well.

I live in a house with my mom, dad, little sister Alison, and little brother Carlo. As you can imagine, we like to do the regular dinosaur things like roar, eat lots of food, and stomp around with our large feet.

I am a tyrannosaurus rex, so my favorite food is meat, though I try to eat lots of vegetables too. I have lots of sharp teeth, and I have to remember to brush them all before I go to bed, or they might fall out.

I am excited because my mom and dad are going out tonight. I am not excited about that part, they are pretty fun to have around, and they always play with me, but it does mean that Uncle Ron is coming to babysit us. Whenever my parents go out, he always comes to look after us, and he is the most fun uncle in the world.

He always calls us little troublemakers, which is funny because we cause almost no trouble at all.

When the knock came at the door, I ran downstairs to greet Uncle Ron. He always does the same knock: knock, knock, knock, then a long silence, then knockety-knock! I always get butterflies in my stomach when I hear that knock because I know that we are about to have lots of fun.

"Uncle Ron!" I shouted as I ran into his arms.

"Hello, troublemaker," said Uncle Ron. See what I said about him calling us troublemakers?

My little brother and little sister followed soon after.

"More troublemakers!" shouted Uncle Ron.

"You kids be good for Uncle Ron," said my dad as he put on his jacket.

"We will," the three of us said together.

"Call me if you need anything," said my mom as she put her hat on.

"We'll be fine," said Uncle Ron. He hugged my mom and closed the door behind her.

"Can we go and do something fun tomorrow?" I asked.

"Woah, I'm just in the door," said Uncle Ron.

"Can we go to the park to play, and have ice cream, and feed the ducks?" I asked.

"Feed the ducks!" shouted Alison. "Can we do that? Can we please. Can we go to the cinema too and get snacks?"

"And play in the arcade, and go to the library, and go for a hike," added Carlo.

"Woah, woah, woah," said Uncle Ron with his arms in the air. "That is a lot of things. Look, tomorrow, I am busy. How about we start tonight with some food? Who wants mac and cheese?"

"I do! I do! I do!" we all shouted together.

"Okay, you go and watch some TV, and I will whip up some dinner," said Uncle Ron.

The three of us went into the living room, and I was just about to switch on the TV when Carlo had a better idea. He suggested that instead of watching a TV show, we should paint a picture for Uncle Ron.

Alison suggested that we paint it on the wall so that it was really big. I thought that was a great idea, so we gathered all the paints that we had and painted a massive picture on the living room wall, with everything that we wanted to do with him. We finished just in time.

"Who wants mac and cheese?" announced Uncle Robert as he walked into the living room, carrying a giant pot of mac and cheese.

As soon as he saw the large painting on the wall, his mouth opened wide. He must have been so surprised at the amazing painting. Then, he dropped the mac and cheese, and it splashed all over the floor.

I tried to help clean it up while Alison and Carlo went off in search of our cleaning bucket.

I really did want to help, but I somehow managed to get the mac and cheese all over the sofa and the rest of the furniture in the room. When Alison and Carlo returned, they had somehow forgotten about the cleaning bucket, had gone out into the yard, and covered themselves in mud. There were now muddy footprints and handprints all over the house.

"Argh!" shouted Uncle Ron.

He's always really funny when he makes that noise. I think that he makes it just to make us laugh because he does it a lot.

"Into the bath!" shouted Uncle Ron. He scooped up Alison, Carlo, and me and took us up to the bathroom, the mac and cheese mixing with the mud as he did.

When we got there, he placed us all down and turned on the faucet. He added a little splash of bubble bath and went to get the towels.

"We need more," said Carlo. He squirted more into the bath.

"That's not how you do it," said Alison. She took the bottle, shook it, and added some more.

"You are doing it wrong," I said, taking the bottle. I added the rest of it to the bath.

When Uncle Ron came back, he could not find us with all the bubbles in the room. The three of us ran out of the bathroom to get some air and went downstairs. Uncle Ron followed us, but he must have forgotten to turn the bathwater off because water started cascading down the stairs like a waterfall.

"NO!" he shouted. "You three wait here while I turn the water off."

Well, we felt bad that Uncle Ron had made such a mess, so we decided to help him. We got the paint from the shed and started to repaint the living room. White was such a boring color, and lime green would look so much better.

When Uncle Ron came back downstairs, we had painted three rooms in lime green, including all of the furniture and the mac and cheese.

I don't think Uncle Ron liked it, but art is very subjective. He put his hands on his head and spun in a circle, looking at the newly-painted rooms.

"Argh!" he shouted again, and the three of us laughed. It was a very funny noise. "Okay, okay, okay," he said. "We need to clean this up. Your parents are going to be home soon."

"They can clean it up," said Carlo. "They are very good at cleaning things up."

"It's true," said Alison.

I wanted to agree with them, but I didn't think that it would help. Instead, I said, "Okay, we'll help you clean up your mess, but you have to do all that fun stuff with us tomorrow."

"Anything," said Uncle Ron.

"Even feeding the ducks?" asked Alison.

"Yes!" said Uncle Ron.

"And the arcade?" asked Carlo.

"Yes, yes, yes, just clean!" he shouted.

We were about to start when we saw our parents pull up in their dinosaur car. We had fifteen seconds to get the house cleaned and repainted. The four of us worked together, cleaning as fast as we could. As my parents opened the door, we wiped the last surface. The house was as clean as it had ever been.

"Did you all have fun?" asked my father.

"Oh, yes," the three of us said.

"Did you all behave for Uncle Ron?" asked my mother.

"We did," the three of us said.

"Can I take them out tomorrow to do something fun?" asked Uncle Ron with a big frown on his face.

The there of us looked at him and smiled.

When Aliens Attack

Mark lay in his bed, and his mom read him a bedtime story. This was his favorite time of the day, and he loved most to hear stories about outer space. His mom would read him stories about space travel, amazing planets, and aliens from other planets.

As his mom read, Mark stared out of the window to the moon and stars above. He wondered if there really were aliens out there, and what they would look like. He reached his hand up to try to touch the stars and quickly recoiled it.

There was dried mud on his hands, and he had to hide them. He had spent most of the day playing in mud, throwing mud, and making delicious mud pies. If his mom saw his muddy hands, she would make him clean them, and clean hands are no fun.

He liked to let the wet mud dry on his hands until it started to crack. Then, he would pretend that he was an alien with weird mud hands.

"The end," said his mom.

Mark had forgotten all about the story and had been too busy imagining what aliens looked like. That didn't matter, he could always ask her to read the story again tomorrow night.

"Goodnight," said Mark.

"Goodnight," said his mom.

"I love you," said Mark.

"I love you too," said his mom. She turned off the light in his room and switched on the nightlight. It was a mini-moon that glowed.

Mark lay in his bed for a long time and eventually fell fast asleep. When he dreamed, he dreamed of aliens and faraway planets. As the sun woke him in the morning, he wiped his eyes with the back of his hands, but he could not get rid of the sleepy feeling.

When Mark opened his eyes, everything felt wrong.

This was not the light of the sun! It was much too bright, and coming from somewhere closer. Mark jumped out of bed and ran to the window, shielding his eyes. It looked like a giant spotlight coming from just above his house.

There was a noise too. It was a deep rumbling that shook the house around him. He had to cling onto the window frame so that he did not lose his balance. He shielded his eyes again and stared up at what was hovering above.

Mark could not believe it.

It was an alien spaceship!

Mark waved to it and tried to shout hello, but there was no response, and it was much too loud to hear anything over the deep rumbling. Suddenly, the noise changed, and more beams of light came from the spaceship. Mark could see that a few spaceships were hovering over the houses in his town.

Then it happened. All of the parents were lifted from their beds and transported up into the spaceships. Mark could hear the other children in his town calling, and he started to shout out too when his mom and dad started to float up to the spaceship.

When all the adults were taken, a funny melody was sounded, and all of the children fell fast asleep.

Mark jumped up when he woke. He could remember everything that had happened the night before. He ran outside and saw the spaceships. They were hovering close to the ground, but they were not doing anything else.

There were children outside too, looking up at the spaceships, and more were coming from houses, shaking themselves awake as they realized that all of the adults had been taken.

Some children think that it would be fun to have no parents around, but it is not much fun when your parents have been taken by aliens.

Mark quickly found his friends.

"Have your parents been taken too?" he asked.

"Yes," said Susan.

"Gone," said Will.
"What are we going to do?" asked Susan.

"I don't know," said Mark. He had the most knowledge of aliens, so the other two waited for him to think of a plan. "We have to attack them," he said finally.

The rallying cry went around, and all of the children grabbed weapons. Some found large rocks, others found tree branches, and a few had metal pipes. Mark had become their unofficial leader.

"Charge!" shouted Mark.

Those with tree branches ran towards the spaceships, getting as close as they could, but they were thrown back by a shield when they touched the ships. It glowed green as they touched it, and it stopped anything from getting through.

"Throw!" shouted Mark.

The rocks came next. Anyone who had a rock threw it at the closest spaceship. Mark watched the rocks arc through the air, and he crossed his fingers. But, when the rocks got within a few inches, the shield activated, and all of the rocks bounced harmlessly away without leaving so much as a dent.

"Final attack!" shouted Mark.

Those with metal pipes ran at the spaceships. This time, they did not get too close and tried to hit the spaceships from a few feet away. They struck down with the metal pipes and poles, hoping to do something but, before the pipes hit, the green shield activated. The pipes were thrown from the children's hands, and they were left standing there with no weapons.

Mark frowned. Not one spaceship had been damaged. The only thing that they had succeeded in doing was to dislodge some dirt that had been clinging to the bottom of the ships. If that was not bad enough, it started to rain.

The children found shelter under trees, and Mark watched the rain bouncing off the spaceships, and he wished that he had weapons made from rain.

"Hey," he said.

"What?" asked Susan.

"Look, the rain is hitting the spaceship and not the shield," said Mark.

"So it is," said Will. "But how does that help us? Are we going to spray water at the spaceships?"

"Not quite," said Mark. "Look at the bottom of the ships. There is some dirt there from when they have landed. Dirt can get through too."

"So, we throw dirt?" asked Susan.

"Almost," said Mark. "We combine the two. If we mix up some mud, we might be able to cover the spaceships in mud. That should do the job."

It was already raining, so it did not take much to turn the dirt into mud. The children formed a production line. Some added more water where needed, others mixed the dirt and water together, and the rest formed the mud into clumps that could be easily thrown.

Mark did the quality control, making sure that the mud was wet enough to stick, large enough to cover a lot of the ship, and light enough to be thrown.

When they had all of the mud weapons assembled, they went to work. The children picked up the mud clumps and threw them at the spaceships. There must have been at least ten thousand mud pies thrown that day.

They threw so much mud that the spaceships started to get heavy and fall slightly towards the ground. When all of the spaceships were completely covered, they heard a noise.

"Please, we surrender!"

Mark raised his hand to stop anyone from throwing any more mud. After a moment, the front of one spaceship opened, followed by the fronts of all the others. The parents walked down the ramps and ran to their kids. Everyone cheered.

As Mark hugged his parents, he looked up into the closest spaceship. There was a large green goo standing there. It did not have a face, but he was sure that it had a frown on its face. Mark waved to it as the door to the spaceship closed.

As quick as they had come, the aliens left Earth. From that day on, all the children of the world kept puddles of mud in their yards just in case the aliens should ever come back.

The Trapped Fairy

Winterbloom flapped her wings and lifted herself through the bright garden. The house lay at the edge of her forest, and whoever lived there took great care of the trees, bushes, and plants.

Winterbloom was a fairy, and she liked to fly through the bright petals and large green leaves in the garden, stopping at the small fish pond to wash her dazzling red wings. Of course, she would never let the human who lived there see her. She knew that there were good humans in the world, but she did not want to risk it. They might keep her as a pet, and that would not be a very good life.

No, she liked to fly free. She was a fairy, after all, and fairies are free beings. They do not want to live as pets, and they rarely live with other fairies. They live by themselves but get together with their friends a lot to have parties and each marigold cupcakes.

Winterbloom lopped in the air and landed on a small bush. Some bright blue berries were growing, and they would soon be ripe enough to pluck and eat. She watched the fish swimming below and wondered what it would be like to live in the water. The fish pond looked much too small for her, and she was glad that she had the entire forest to live in.

She picked one of the berries and ate it. It was a little sweet, but she would not pick any more, not just yet. She was about to turn around and fly back into the forest when she smelled the most delicious smell. It was a similar smell to the berry, but much sweeter.

A glance towards the house and she could see what was causing the aroma. On the kitchen windowsill, there was a pie, fresh from the oven. Whoever lived there must have baked it with the same berries from the garden.

Winterbloom hovered closer and found her mouth-watering. She thought about taking a bite from the pie or sampling just a little bit of it, but she might get caught doing it, and it was not hers to take. Instead, she sat on the windowsill for a while and smelled the delicious smell.

"Mmm, that smells so nice," said Winterbloom.

She was about to fly away when she caught sight of the inside of the house. She had looked through the window before, but she had never been so close to the inside. There were so many cool things to look at.

There were large seats with cushions on the top. She had a small chair in her tiny house, but it was nothing like this one. There was also a place in the wall to have a fire. Winterbloom jumped up and down.

"Whoever heard of having a fire inside your home," she whispered.

She was about to leave, even though there were so many fascinating things when she saw something that deserved a closer look.

"I really shouldn't go inside," whispered Winterbloom, "but I have to."

She had spotted a painting on the wall. In the painting, there were lots of daisies, and, below the daisies, fairies were dancing. The fairies did not look exactly like fairies look in real life, but they were pretty close. Winterbloom wondered if a human had seen a fairy before.

Before she knew what she was doing, she found herself flying into the house. She flew straight to the picture on the wall and examined all of the beautiful colors. In the picture, the fairies were all dancing, and Winterbloom felt like dancing too.

Swoosh!

Winterbloom turned around and froze. There was a woman who stood at the window with her back to her. The woman had closed the window and was lifting up the pie. As she turned around, Winterbloom flattened herself against the painting and made herself look like she was dancing.

The woman looked straight at the painting, shook her head as if she were imagining things, and walked away towards the kitchen.

Winterbloom let out a sigh of relief. She let her heartbeat slow and flew back over to the window. It was closed all the way. She tried to lift it up, but it was too heavy. She was stuck in the house. Winterbloom knew that she had to get out of there before she was spotted.

She could not hear the woman, so she looked around. There were no other windows in the room, and the only door was where the woman had gone.

"There is the fireplace!" whispered Winterbloom in delight. She flew over to it, perched herself on the logs, and looked up. It was completely black. She flew up a little way, but there was no way out, it was blocked entirely by soot.

Winterbloom sneezed, and a cloud of black soot flew up around her. When she came back out of the fireplace, she no longer had red wings. They were mostly black with specks of red. Most of her body was covered in black. She looked like a bat.

"Well, I guess that I have no other option," said Winterbloom.

There was only one thing to do, and that was to leave the living room and try to find a way out. She visited a few rooms but did not find anything useful.

One room had large books all over the walls, but there was no time to sit in there and read.

Another room had a large container that looked like it might be another pond, but there was a hole in the bottom. Water dripped from a metal pipe and ran down the hole. There was a smaller container that almost looked like a seat. There was a small amount of water in the bottom of it, and Winterbloom drank some of it. She was very thirsty.

The next room had lots of food in it, but some was in a very cold box, and Winterbloom almost got herself trapped in there. She would not have minded that for there were many delicious cakes and other sweet treats in there.

She would have stayed in there is she had not heard the scream.

"Aargh!!!! A bat!" screamed the woman.

"I'm a fairy," said Winterbloom indignantly, though the woman did not understand what she said. Humans cannot speak the fairy language.

Winterbloom had only just looked up when a broom came crashing down towards her head. She flapped her wings and took to the air. The woman screamed some more, and blindly swung the broom around her head in large circles.

Winterbloom flew from room to room, but there were no open windows or doors. She wondered why the woman was so angry. Had she never seen a fairy before? Winterbloom flew back to the window and tried to open it, but she could not. There were tiny fairy footprints and handprints all across the house.
When all seemed lost, the woman threw open the front door and shouted, "Shoo!"

Winterbloom had heard that word before, and thought that is must have meant something like, "I have opened the door for you, you are welcome to leave."

So, she did. Winterbloom flew past the woman, waved at her as she did, and flew from the house. When she was outside, she gave a little laugh. It had been a fun adventure, especially with how ridiculous the woman had looked swinging the broom around her head.

From that day forth, Winterblloom never went into another house ever again, no matter how nice it smelled.

The Boy With No Birthday

Once, there was a boy who had no birthday. No one knew how old he was, and no matter how much he searched, he could not find his birthday.

"Mom, when is my birthday?" asked the boy.

"I don't remember," said his mom. "I think that it might be sometime in November."

"Dad, do you know when my birthday is?" asked the boy.

"Hmm," replied his dad. "I think that it might be on a Wednesday."

"Grandma, when was I born?" asked the boy.

"I think that it might have been in 2012," said his grandma with a hoarse whisper.

"Grandpa, you must know when my Birthday is," said the boy, a little exasperated at not being able to find his birthday.

"The moon!" shouted his grandpa. That really did not help.

So, the boy was left to look for his birthday on his own. He could not remember being born, that would be ridiculous. He tried to remember as far back as he could, but he could not remember anything from his youth. It had been a long time since his youth, almost two years, and he could not remember that far back.

He might remember a birthday party, but he was not sure if it was his. He would have to do some more detective work.

The boy went to his closet. He remembered getting some presents, but that could have been from Christmas, it was hard to tell. He searched through his closet and found some toys that he had received recently, but there were no clues there.

He got a little distracted and decided to play with his toys for a little while. He built with his blocks, building a large tower. After that, he lined up his toy soldiers and knocked them over with his Nerf gun. Then, he tried to stack all of his soft toys as big as he could, and he followed that up by building a large fort.

It was only when he found a piece of wrapping paper that he remembered about his mission. He was supposed to be looking for his birthday, and he had forgotten all about it. No wonder he had forgotten his birthday if this was how easily he got distracted.

"Hmm," said the boy, flipping the paper over and over in his hands. He could see the letter 'b 'on it, and there were no Christmas images, only a star, and a soccer ball. "I'm sure that this is from my birthday, so that proves that I do have a birthday. I just need to find out when it is."

The boy was tempted to play some more in his fort, but he had more important things to do. He walked downstairs and put on his jacket and hat.

"I'm going out," he said. "I'll be back soon." He had some people to visit.

First, he went to his other grandparents, who lived down the street. They were very sensible people and would surely know when his birthday was. If he only knew, he could discover how old he was, and begin to plan for his next birthday.

The boy knocked on the door, and his grandmother answered.

"Come in, come in," she said.

"Grandma, do you know when my birthday is?" asked the boy when he was inside.

"I think that I do," replied the grandma. "You know, that reminds me of the time when I went to Berlin. I was there for a work conference, very boring, it was all about elephants and how they can dance. Anyway, I was walking down the street when I bumped into an old friend of mine. She told me a story about the time she went boating in the Atlantic ocean and ran into pirates, very boring stuff. Still, it reminded her of the time that she had to answer the telephone, and that part is very interesting. You should pay attention now because it is all about school work."

The boy's grandma could really talk, and she often said a lot without saying anything at all. So, the boy let her talk while he asked his grandpa if he knew when his birthday was.

"Do you know when my birthday is, Grandpa?" asked the boy.

"Have you checked up your nose?" asked his grandpa.
The boy had not checked up his nose, but he was sure that it was not up there. How could it be? Well, he had come here to get some sensible answers, but it would seem that adults could be very silly when they wanted to be.

"I have to go," said the boy.

"But you have not even had any cakes yet," said his grandma.

"Well, maybe I could stay for that," said the boy. There were some things in life that were a little more important than finding out when your birthday was, and cake was one of those things.

When the boy had a stomach full of cakes, he went off in search of his friends. If anyone was going to remember when his birthday was, they surely would.

Karen was already playing on the street. She was whizzing up and down on her scooter.

"Karen, do you know when my birthday is?" asked the boy.

"Your birthday?" asked Karen, a little surprised. "No, I have no idea. Oh, look at the time. I have to go." She whizzed away.

The boy knocked on Lucas's door next.

"Lucas, when is my birthday?" asked the boy.

"Is this a trick question?" asked Lucas. He closed the door, and the boy was left standing there alone.

There was one friend left to try, his best friend. If anyone was going to know, it would be Lily.

"Lily," said the boy when he finally caught up to her. She was running down the street. "When is my birthday?"

"No time, got to go," said Lily. She ran away as fast as she could.

The boy did not know what to do. He had lost his birthday, and he did not think that he would ever find it. He had nothing else to do but go home.

"Maybe I will stay the same age forever," said the boy.
When he got home, he was feeling sad, and he hung his head down and put on a frown to make himself look extra sad. He opened the door and walked into his house.

"Surprise!" shouted everyone.

The boy looked up with a big smile on his face. He had found his birthday. His parents were there. All his grandparents were there. All of his friends were there. He was not sure how he had done it, but he had found it.

This time, he was not going to lose it again. He looked at the calendar. January 7th. He opened his personal notebook and grabbed a pen to write the date down. On the first page, in big, bold letters, was the words:

January 7th: BIRTHDAY!

The words were underlined six times. He underlined them one more time.

"That should help me to remember," whispered the boy.

He put the book back in his pocket and enjoyed the birthday party, There were lots of presents, and he tore the wrapping off of them excitedly. His grandma had brought lots of cake with her, and he found room to put more cakes in his belly. There were even fun games and dancing. When the party was done, the boy was happier than he had ever been.

His friends said goodbye, and everyone left. The boy sat on the couch with a belly full of cake.

"Now," he said to himself. "I just need to find out what my name is."

The Baby That Could Not Sleep

There once was a baby that could not sleep. No matter what anyone did, the baby would not sleep. When it was time for bed, the baby would be put into its crib, and then it would start to cry. It would cry and cry and cry.

"Waaaaaaaaaaaaaaaaaaaaaaaaa!" shouted the baby as it lay down in its crib.

"Oh, no," said his mother. "We need to do something." She quickly ran around the house with her hands on her head, humming an exasperated tune. She was sure that she had all of her baby books only a few minutes ago, and now they all seemed to be missing. She looked under the couch cushions, in the bathtub, and she even searched through the freezer. She hung her head in shame when she could not find them.

When she got back to the baby room, she remembered that she had left them beside the baby crib. She let out a little laugh and picked up the first book. The baby cried even louder.

"Waaaaaaaaaaaaaaaaaaaaaaaaa!" shouted the baby.

His mother opened the first book and read it as quickly as she could. When she was done reading the book, the baby was crying even louder. So, she opened another book. This one was about a nice dragon and really was a wonderful story. But, when she was done, the baby was only crying more. So, she tried a third. This book was about trees that dance, and the mother was sure that it would help her baby. When she was done, the baby was crying more.

"Waaaaaaaaaaaaaaaaaaaaaaaaa!" screamed the baby.

"I don't know what to do," said the mother.

"I think that I know what needs to be done," said the baby's father. "He is just not calm enough to sleep. I am going to give him a bath."

The father ran off and put some water in the bath. He added cold water first, then some hot, then some cold to make it cool again. He needed to add some hot water after that because he had made it too cold again. Then it was too hot, then too cold, then too hot, then too cold, then too hot, then it was just right.

He ran back to the bedroom and picked up the crying baby. He unwrapped the blanket, took off the baby onesie, pulled off the tiny socks, removed the diaper (thankfully it was empty), and placed the baby gently in the bath.

"Coo, coo, coo, coo," sang his father.

He scooped up some water and ran it over the baby's head. He added some shampoo and washed the hair before rinsing it. He washed between the baby's toes and in the crooks of his elbows. He even washed the baby's bum. When the baby was as clean as a baby can get, his father removed him from the water.

He dried the baby from head to toe, even getting into the spaces between the toes. He put some powder on the baby and put on a fresh diaper (it would not stay fresh for long). He put the tiny socks back on and the baby onesie. He wrapped the blanket around the baby, and placed the baby back in the crib, placing a hundred stuffed toys around his baby boy.

The baby cried louder.

"Waaaaaaaaaaaaaaaaaaaaaaaaa!" cried the baby.

"No, no," said the baby's oldest sister. "He is unhappy because he wants to play. Once he had played, he will go to sleep."

She picked up one of the toys and danced it in front of the baby's face. The teddy bear danced from side to side as the baby cried.

A stuffed penguin was chosen next. The penguin hopped up and down on the baby's belly. The oldest sister made it sing as it danced around the crib.

Next up were a lion and a tiger dancing together. The oldest sister gave them voices and made them sing to each other as they danced around the crib.

The oldest sister juggled three of the stuffed bird toys next, but that did not help to calm the baby. He only cried louder.

"Waaaaaaaaaaaaaaaaaaaaaaaaaa!" he cried louder than before.

The oldest sister tried to make the animals talk to her baby brother. She made the animals tell him that he was safe now and that it was time to sleep, and they would be there to protect him. But, no matter what she did, her baby brother cried. And, it seemed that the more that she tried to calm him, the louder her cried.

"Waaaaaaaaaaaaaaaaaaaaaaaaa!" cried the baby, even louder than he had before.

"I know what to do," said the baby's older brother. He was only five years old, but he already had lots of great ideas. "He needs some human interaction."

His parents had no idea where he had heard the words *human interaction*, but there were willing to try anything. They watched as the older brother picked up the baby and held him to his shoulder. He slowly bounced the baby up and down on his shoulder.

"Waaaaaaaaaaaaaaaaaaaaaaaaa!" cried the baby.

He sang a sweet song into his ear, moving slowly around the room, being the best big brother in the world. His older sister watched. His parents watched. The baby even seemed to watch before he started to cry again.

"Waaaaaaaaaaaaaaaaaaaaaaaaa!" screamed the baby. If it were possible, the baby was crying even louder than before, and it was crying pretty loudly before. Everyone in the room wondered how something so small could make so much noise.

"Waaaaaaaaaaaaaaaaaaaaaaaaa!" the baby cried again.

The older brother patted his baby brother on the back and told him that it was going to be okay. He put his face in front of his baby brother's face and made reassuring noises. He tried pulling funny faces to make his brother laugh, but that did not work. No matter what he did, no matter what anyone did, the baby only continued to cry.

"Waaaaaaaaaaaaaaaaaaaaaaaaa!" the baby cried.

"There is only one thing that we can do," said the father. "We have to work together. We should all sing a lullaby together, and that will surely calm him. If we do that, we will surely soothe him."

"What about Lavender?" asked the older brother. Lavender was the youngest girl in the house, but she was already fast asleep. She was two years old, and a very good sleeper. Her baby brother had not followed in her footsteps.

"It will just have to be the four of us," said the father.

So, the four of them agreed on which song to sing, and they began to sing it. The song is a beautiful song, but they did not sing it beautifully. They were awful singers, and they were even worse when they sang together. It was the worst thing that had ever been heard in the history of the world.

You can guess what happened next. Yes, the baby began to cry even louder.

"Waaaaaaaaaaaaaaaaaaaaaaaaaa!" cried the baby as loud as it could.

"What are you all doing?" asked Lavender. She was stood in the doorway of the baby room with a sleepy expression on her face.

"We are trying to calm your baby brother," said her mother. "He won't stop crying."

"Waaaaaaaaaaaaaaaaaaaaaaaaaa!" cried the baby.

"Well, no wonder," said Lavender. "I would be the same if I had so many people fussing over me. You should leave him alone to sleep."

"Leave him alone," said her mother.

"Huh," said her father.

"That's an idea," said her older brother.

"Maybe we could try it," said her older sister.

So, the four of them left the room, and, three minutes later, there was no sound from the room. The baby had fallen fast asleep.

The Weird Guy

Bill was a very weird guy.

He did not like to sleep in a bed like most regular people do. He does not have a comfortable mattress like you and me, nor does he have a nice soft pillow to rest his head on. You might think that he has a warm blanket to curl up under when it gets cold, but you would be wrong.

Bill has a solid wooden board that he sleeps on. He likes to have a solid wooden board because it is good for his back. It helps to keep his back straight when he is sleeping, and that makes him happy. Of course, if he flips onto his stomach, then his belly becomes straight instead, but he does not mind this.

In place of a pillow, Bill paces his head on a cat. Cats are very soft, and this cat will wake Bill in the morning, so he does not need an alarm clock. The cat likes Bill, so he tolerates having a large head on him.

While most people like to have a blanket or comforter to keep themselves warm during the night, Bill uses a sleeping bag. He found that blankets are so often knocked off the bed during the night, so he zips himself up inside a sleeping bag so that only his eyes are showing. Bill is never cold during the night, and this makes him happy.

When morning comes, and the cat meows, Bill knows that it is time to get up. It is much better to be woken by a friendly cat that it is to be woken by a loud alarm clock, and you do not have to turn off a cat, so this saves Bill three seconds every morning. Bill likes to save time. It makes him happy.

Bill heard a scientist talking on the radio one afternoon, and the scientist claimed that it is better to brush your teeth with charcoal than with toothpaste, so that is exactly what Bill does every morning. He does not use toothpaste to brush his teeth, he uses charcoal. His teeth might be black by the time he is done, but he has never had any cavities, and this makes Bill happy.

Bill has always wondered why there is breakfast food. You can eat lunch food for dinner, and dinner food for lunch, but why is breakfast food eaten at breakfast. I mean, you can eat breakfast food for dinner and snacks, but you wouldn't eat dinner for breakfast. *You* wouldn't, but Bill would.

Bill had never really been one for cereal and toast. He liked them occasionally but did not want to have them every morning. He much preferred roast dinners. For breakfast this morning, he cooked himself up a roast chicken, Brussels sprouts, roast potatoes, corn, and gravy. When he was done, he had pumpkin pie for breakfast dessert. This made Bill happy.

When you work in an office, you usually wear a suit. Can you guess who does not wear a suit when he works in an office? Bill did wear a suit for the first couple of days but soon grew tired of it. When he turned up to work in shorts and a t-shirt, he got some funny stares.

He was even called into his boss's office and given a good talking to. A good talking to is never usually very good and is usually bad, which is weird. Maybe there are more weird people in this world than just Bill.

Anyway, Bill's boss could not help but agree that Bill still did his work, no matter what he was wearing. In fact, it was probably true that Bill did more work when he was wearing his shorts and t-shirt. He was not restricted by a tie or tight pants, or a stuffy shirt or jacket. When he was freed of that unnecessary clothing, he could work harder and smarter.

There was some talk of everyone wearing shorts and t-shirts to work, and this made Bill happy.

I should also tell you about how Bill says hello and goodbye.

Bill does not say hello, he says, "Howdy-diddly-doody."

Bill does not say goodbye, he says, "See ya later, Tater."

This gets him some funny looks when he says it, and people think that he is extra weird. Yet, once they walk away, they cannot help but feel a smile come to their faces. If Bill knew how much his words made people happy, he would be even happier.

When it is your birthday, anniversary, or some other special occasion, you probably won't get a present from Bill. He likes to give presents at random times of the year, and he gives presents because he likes people or they have done something special.

You won't get a present on Christmas, but you might get one on June 9th. You also won't get a present because it has been a certain number of years since you were born, but you might get one if you work hard to help people who have a hard life. People always expect presents at certain times of the year, but it is much more fun to get a present when you are not expecting it.

On his lunch break, Bill likes to go for a run. But, he does not run like everyone else. He does not want to waste time running for a long time, so he runs as fast as he can for as long as he can. When he cannot run anymore, he walks back to the office and has his lunch.

Sometimes, for lunch, he will have a big slice of cake and some ice cream. Sometimes he will have asparagus dipped in ketchup. Occasionally, he will have a slice of lamb with peanut butter on it. He will eat whatever he wants to eat. He thinks people who eat things that they don't want to eat are weird.

Bill also has a pet, thought the bird does not know that it is a pet. When the bird visited his yard one day to eat some seed, Bill took a liking to it. He had always thought it weird that people buy animals and then keep them in their houses—no wonder those animals spend so much time trying to get out.

Bill named the bird Tweeter. It visits his yard every day, and Bill holds out his hand full of seed for the bird to land on and eat. Sometimes other birds come too, and that is fine because they are friends of his pet bird. Tweeter is the best pet that he has ever owned. I should mention that the cat he uses as a pillow is not his pet. It wandered into his house one day and never left.

Before bed, Bill likes to fill a basin with jello and stick his feet into it. Why does he do this? Because it feels good. It also makes his feet smell like lemon or strawberry or peaches. The cat seems to like it too and will lick his feet clean. It tickles and makes him laugh.

At bedtime, Bill will read himself a bedtime story. There is no one else around to do it, so he has to do it himself. He always chooses a good story and reads it well, doing all of the voices. While he reads, he has grapes and milk. He likes to dip the grapes into the milk.

When he gets into bed, he stretches five times before zipping up his sleeping bag. As he falls asleep, he always smiles.

Some people might think that he is weird, but Bill is almost certainly the happiest person in the world.

How To Calm Your Mind

Sometimes it can be hard to relax.

There are times when you get into bed, and you just cannot switch off your mind. You might have had something exciting happen during the day, and you cannot stop thinking about it, or you might have something that is worrying you, and you cannot get it out of your head.

It can be hard to have worries, and it can be very hard to stop thinking about them. There are times when, no matter what you do, you cannot get rid of the worries from your mind.

Even if you have something fun and exciting in your mind, it can cause you trouble if you cannot sleep.

When we go to sleep, it gives our minds some time to rest, and that is very important for everyone. When you cannot sleep, your mind cannot rest, and then all of your problems can get worse.

When you sleep, your brain has time to process all of the information that it has collected over the day, and you usually collect a lot of information. It is also a time when your brain deals with problems.

Have you ever had a problem that you could not solve or a problem that was causing you a lot of trouble, and felt sad about it? Have you ever gone to sleep and felt better about it in the morning? That is because your brain can help to solve your problems when you are sleeping.

It doesn't even matter if you solve the problem or not, after sleeping, you usually feel better about any problems that you may have. Sleep is a wonderful thing, and it is very important.

So, when it is hard to sleep, not only does your body feel more tired, your brain does too. If you cannot sleep well, your problems are going to seem worse than they are, and you are never going to solve them.

This story is here to help you to switch off your brain and get to sleep. When that happens, all of your problems are going to diminish. This means that they are not going to be as bad as they first seem. They might still be problems, but big problems will shrink into small problems, and small problems will pop like balloons.

Balloons are important for this, so get ready to think about lots of different balloons.

Everyone has problems, so we are going to start with your problems and get them out of the way so that you can sleep. The best part is that you do not have to talk about your problems if you do not want to, but it is always better to share a problem is you can. When you share a problem, it cuts it in half immediately, and the person who you tell it to can often help.

Okay, back to clearing your mind.

Make sure that you are comfortable in your bed and close your eyes.

If you need to get any wiggles out of the way, do it now. Shake your body, wriggle your toes and fingers, get all of that energy out of your body, and relax.

With your eyes closed, you are going to think of a big problem. What big problem did you encounter today? It can be anything that you want. If it is a big problem for you, then it is a big problem, and do not let anyone tell you otherwise.

Now, think about that big problem and how it makes you feel. It probably doesn't feel good, does it? That is okay, problems do not make anyone feel good.

Now, imagine this problem in your mind. It might take the form of the problem. Maybe your problem is about sharing, and you can imagine not sharing or having someone not share with you. Think about a specific incident if you can.

If there is not a specific incident, then think of how you feel. Maybe you are sad, but don't know why. What does that sadness look like? Does it look like a big blue cloud, a scary snake, something else?

Think of an image that represents your problem. Now, add all the emotion to that image, and hold it in your mind.

Get ready to scream!

We are not going to scream out loud, we are going to scream in our minds. In your mind, take a balloon. It is not blown up yet, but it soon will be. Put the ballon to your mouth and, in your mind, scream into it. Scream about your big problem, filling up the balloon. As you scream in your mind, the balloon will get bigger and bigger, but it does not burst.

When you have screamed all of your problem, let go of the balloon. It will magically tie itself in front of you. Your problem is still there, but it is now inside the balloon. Imagine the balloon in your mind. How big is it? What shape is it? What color is it?

The balloon floats in front of you, and it is now time to send it deep into your mind so that your brain can work on it while you sleep.

As you keep your eyes closed, you find that you have a massive pin in your hand. It is very sharp at one end, and the point glistens in the light. When you are ready, bring up the pin and stab it into the balloon. As you do, the balloon burst with a big 'POP! 'and the problem disappears from your mind.

Good job, you are helping yourself to become a better person.

Now, we are going to do the same with your next big problem. Think about it in your mind, imagine what it looks like, scream it into a balloon, and pop that balloon when you are ready. Do this for as many big problems as you have.

After this, you can concentrate on the smaller problems. Are there any things that have made you frustrated, angry, or sad, but you shouldn't really be annoyed by them? Maybe you didn't get ice cream after dinner, or someone stepped on your toe, or the sun wasn't shining today. It doesn't matter what it is, if it is a problem for you, then it is a valid problem.

Now, we are going to take all of those small problems and scream them into the same balloon, in your mind, of course.

Think about all of the problems together. Imagine as many of them as you can, think about how you feel, imagine shapes, colors, and anything else that comes to mind. When you have them all there, scream them all into a big balloon. This is going to be the biggest balloon ever. Keep screaming (in your mind) until you have filled the balloon with all of your problems.

How does it feel to have this giant balloon in front of you? What size is it? What shape is it? What color is it?

Are you ready to pop it?

Tale the large needle in your hand, and stick it into the balloon. Can you hear the large 'POP! 'as you burst it. Feels good, doesn't it? Let the problems be sent to the back of your mind so that your brain can deal with them while you sleep.

Your problems are still there, but you do not need to worry about them for a while, your brain will do that while you sleep.

Before you open your eyes, let go of the pin. When you do, it turns into birds. The birds fly away into the distance until you cannot see them anymore. When they are gone, your mind is blank, a safe space for you to be.

If you want to go to sleep, go to sleep now. If you are not ready, slowly open your eyes, and continue to relax.

Goodnight.

The Musical Animals

Lynne was a fox. The one thing that she loved to do more than anything in the world was to play her guitar. She would play it when she got up in the morning, and she would play it before she went to bed. She would also play it all of the time between getting up and going to bed.

She had been playing for as long as she could remember, and had gotten really good. She had practiced every day to become as good as she was, and continued to practice every day so that she got even better.

When you are good at something, you always need to keep practicing at it.

So, this is exactly what he did. Lynne practiced playing lots of different songs every day, and she was happy that she could play the guitar so well.

"But, I think that I could be better," said Lynne. "Yet, I don't know how."

"You already play so well," said her friend Roxy. "You could learn to play new songs."

"I have learned lots of new songs, but I think that something else is missing," said Lynne.

"What if you played a different instrument?" asked Roxy.

"No," said Lynne. "I like the guitar so much," said Lynne.

" Then, I don't know what," said Roxy.

"Me neither," said Lynne. "I'm going to go for a walk.

When Lynne went for a walk, she took her guitar with her. She always took her guitar everywhere. As she walked, she sang her favorite songs, creating a merry melody in the forest. As she wandered, she thought about what was missing from her playing. She was not sure that she could get any better on the guitar.

Bang! Bang! Dunk! Thunk! Boom, boom, boom! Krsh! Badoom!

Lynne liked the beat immediately. Someone was playing the drums. As Lynne listened, the drumbeat moved from fast to slow and back to fast again. At first, it seemed like there was no pattern to it, but Lynne soon found the pattern, and she started to play along.

As she got closer, she played louder, and the two instruments started to work in harmony. When Lynne was really close, the drumbeat stopped. Lynne stopped too.

A Squirrel popped its head out from the trunk of a tree.

"Oh, it's you," said Sandy, the squirrel.

"It's me," said Lynne.

"I have no idea who you are, but I like your guitar playing," said Sandy. "Do you want to play some more together?"

"Yes, please," said Lynne. "You are so good at playing the drums."

"I know," replied Sandy.

The two of them played together for hours, and Lynne found a little of what was missing from her life. She loved to play by herself, but playing with someone else made her own playing even better.

Sandy played the drums, and Lynne joined in with her own song. Then they swapped. Lynne started the beat, and Sandy joined in. They were amazing together.

"Hello?" A voice stopped them playing. Lynne and Sandy looked up to see a bear with a banjo.

"Can I play too?" asked Roland, the bear.

"Are you any good?" asked Sandy. "You have to be good to play with us."

"I don't know," said Roland.

"Of course you can play," said Lynne. "Don't listen to Sandy."

Roland walked over and stood beside Lynne. He held his banjo but did not say anything. Sandy did not waste any time and started banging on his drums. Lynne soon joined in, but Roland was a little more shy. It was not until Lynne smiled at him and nodded that he started to play.

Lynne was glad that he had turned up. As soon as Roland started playing his banjo, his fingers were a blur. He played so fast that Sandy could almost not keep up on the drums.

"This boy can play!" shouted Sandy when they had played their first song together.

As they played together, Sandy found a little more of what she was looking for. She realized that she needed people to share her music with. This was what would bring her joy. So, she put up adverts all around the forest.

It did not take long for lots more animals to join them in their jam sessions.

A snake came along with an accordion. There were three mice with trumpets. A wolf played the oboe. Two crocodiles played bass guitar. An owl sang lead vocals. Nine beavers sang backup vocals. A spider played the tuba. A bumblebee had a flute. The elephant was the last to join, he played the triangle.

When Lynne turned up to the jam session, she was excited to see so many animals with instruments.

"This is not going to work," said Sandy.

"It will work, just have a little faith," said Lynne.

Sandy beat the snare drum, starting a count, and all the animals joined in at the same time. Lynne almost stopped playing. She could see Roland smiling beside her, and he was just amazed as she was. They had never played all together before, yet they played with each other perfectly.

As Lynne smiled at Roland, she found some more of what she was looking for. She had been playing alone for so long, but she had so many musical friends now. Yet, there was still something missing. She was not sure, though, if they could fit in any more musicians.

When Lynne went home that night, she was happier than she had ever been, but she was still frustrated. She had found everything that she had been looking for, people to share her music with, but she still felt that something was missing.

"Why am I still unhappy when I am so happy?" Lynne whispered as she fell asleep that night.

The next day, she went back to the agreed practice spot and found most of the animals there. Roland was directing them. They were placing logs and branches on the ground, moving rocks, and flattering some grass.

"What is going on?" asked Lynne.

"You are not fully happy," said Roland.

"I am happy," claimed Lynne.

"No, I could see it in your smile yesterday," said Roland. "You are happy, but not fully happy, and I know why."

"Why?" asked Lynne. "She hoped that he had the answers that she was struggling to find.

"You want to share your music, right?" asked Roland.

"Yes, and I can do that with all of you," replied Lynne.

"But it is not enough," said Roland. "It is not enough for any of us. We want to share our music too, and not just with other musicians. We want to share it with everyone. That is why I put up all of these posters last night, with Sandy's help, of course."

Sandy was sitting in a tree branch and smiling.

Lynne looked at the poster. It was advertising a concert that was scheduled to happen in twenty minutes. It did not take long for all of the animals in the forest to turn up and take their seats.

Before Lynne could question what was happening, Sandy counted them in, and all of the animals started playing and singing. Lynne was caught up in it, and could not stop herself from playing.

The concert lasted for four hours, and the audience went crazy at the end, demanding an encore. Lynne and her band played for another hour. When they were done, everyone asked when the next concert would be. Lynne promised that it would be soon.

With the help of Sandy and Roland, Lynne had found everything that she had ever dreamed of.

The Oil Fountain

In the land of the robots, life was hard. Not that it was purposely hard, it just happened to be hard.

Robots are made out of metal, and that can make things difficult.

If you are made from skin and bones, like you and I are, some things are easy. Wait, I should not presume things. You are made from skin and bones, aren't you? Anyway, going out in the rain is no problem for the likes of us, not so for robots.

Because robots are made from metal, they cannot go out in the rain, or they might rust. They can, however, step on a nail and not have it hurt them. You do not want to step on a nail, believe me, it is not pleasant.

Rick was only two years old when he wanted to go and play in the rain.

"Go out! Go out! Go out!" he chanted.

"No, no, no," said his mother. "You cannot go out in this rain, or you will rust. That happened to your aunt Jane. She got caught in the rain, and she still cannot move her left leg."

When Rick was four, he started to ask more questions.

"Why can't we go out in the rain? It rains so much. Why does it rain so much, and why can't we go out in the rain?" asked Rick.

"If we get caught in the rain," said his mother, "we will start to rust. When that happens, it makes it hard for us to move, and there is no cure for that, just ask your Aunt Jane. As for why it rains so much, that I do not know. Now, go and play and stop worrying."

When he was six, he still could not understand why it rained so much.

"Why do we live in a world where rain makes us rust?" he asked.

No one had an answer for that.

When he was eight, he tried asking more questions.

"There surely must be a way to stop us from rusting, shouldn't there?" asked Rick.

"Not that I know of," replied his mother.

"There is the fountain of youth," spat his grandmother, an old clanky robot that sat in a metal rocking chair in the corner.

"Oh, mother," said Rick's mom. "Not this again."

"What is the fountain of youth?" asked Rick.

"It was a legend that my grandmother told me when I was a little girl. Somewhere there is a fountain that will keep you young," said his grandmother.

"It would have been found by now," said Rick's mom.

"It's in the Rainy Plains," said his grandmother.

"Where?" asked Rick.

"A place that you must never go," said Rick's mother.

"Your mother is right," said his grandmother. "It is a very dangerous place. It is a place where it rains almost all of the time. It is said that the fountain of youth is there."

"Why would it be in such a dangerous place?" asked Rick.

"Anything worth anything is usually hard to get," said his grandmother.

"But, why?" asked Rick.

"I don't know," said his grandmother. "That's just the way that things are sometimes."

"I would go," said Aunt Jane. She was stood in the corner looking out the window. "If I could." Ever since she had been caught in the rain a second time, both of her legs had seized up, and she could not sit down anymore.

When Rick turned nine, he had finally had enough. His Aunt Jane had been caught in the rain two more times, and she could only move her head now. Rick was not sure how she continued to smile. Maybe her lips had been rusted into a permanent smile.

Rick packed his adventure bag and headed for the Rainy Plains. When he got there, he stopped dead. There was rain falling, and he did not dare to get any closer. He pulled a nuts&bolts bar from his bag and chomped down on it.

He pulled his flashlight from his bag and pointed it at the Rainy Plains. That did nothing to help him. He pulled out a pen and paper. The Rainy Plains looked extensive, and there was a lot of rain. He had to be careful. He would do his best to map out the entire place.

When the rain finally stopped, he readied himself. He was about to run into the Rainy Plains when it started to rain again. He stopped running just in time and did not get wet.

When the rain stopped for a second time, he waited for a minute. When he started running, the rain started again, and he had to turn back.

He vowed to go for it as soon as the rain stopped.

When it stopped a third time, he took off running, moving between the trees that lined the Rainy Plains. He tried to map the area as much as he could. When there was an eruption of thunder, he quickly turned back. He had only just made it back out when the rain started again.

"A good start," he said. He had started his map, and he would be able to make it farther the next time.

When the next time came, he ran as fast as he could, drawing his map and looking for shelter. He spotted a rocky overhang in the distance but had already spent too much time in there. He turned back and ran out. The rain started soon after.

It rained for a long time and, when it stopped, Rick ran as fast as he could. He only just made it to the rocky overhang when the rain splashed down. Two seconds more and he would have been caught.

"No turning back," said Rick. He did not know if the fountain of youth was a real fountain, nor what it would be like, but he did know that if he got caught in the rain, he would never leave this place, and no one would come to rescue him.
When the rain stopped, he continued the adventure, this time from the rocky overhang. He darted back and forth, mapping out the area, and hoping to get closer to the fountain. When he found a cave, that became his new stopping point.

This time, his flashlight was useful. As he shone it into the dark cave, he saw some writing on the wall.

When you leave this cave, do not turn tail.
Keep moving, and you will prevail.
Move towards the mountain.
There you will find the fountain.

Rick knew what he had to do. He did not know how he knew, but he had the feeling that the fountain would save him from the rain. He had to believe that the words were meant for him.

"It's now or never," he said.

The rain stopped.

Rick ran.

He ran as fast as he could. He ran directly towards the mountain. After fifteen seconds, his mind told him to go back, but his heart kept his legs moving. He ran up the hill, and the rain started.

There it was!

In the distance, a fountain spurting black liquid into the air. The rain fell on him, but he could not stop. He could feel his arms seizing up. They hung unmoving at his sides as he continued to run.

His legs began to feel it. They were seizing up too. He was so close that he could smell it. It was the most wonderful aroma in the world. He was so close when his left leg seized up. He hopped as fast as he could, almost able to touch it. With his last ounce of strength, as his entire body seized up, he hopped one last hop and fell into the fountain.

It took a second, but the fountain of oil slowly lubricated all of his joints. It was still raining, but, after a few seconds, he could move freely.

Rick scooped up as much as he could in an empty container and walked out of the Rainy Plains. Everyone was amazed to see him. He went to his Aunt Jane first and lubricated her joints.

From that day forward, everyone visited the oil fountain, and no robot ever feared the rain again.

The Most Beautiful Flower In The World

"Remind me again?" asked Jessica. "Where are we going?"

"We are on an adventure," said her father.

"Yes, I know that," said Jessica. "But why are we on this adventure?"

"We are hunting for the most beautiful flower in the world," said her father.

"And, we cannot see it at home?" asked Jessica,

"No!" stated her father, astonished that she would even think such a thing. "There is only one place that the flower grows, and it only blooms once every hundred years. No one in our lifetime has ever seen it."

"Sounds pretty cool," said Jessica.

"It is cool," stammered her father. "It is cool. It will be cool. I hope that it is cool." He whispered the last part.

Jessica left him to his thoughts. She had been traveling for four days with her family, and there were still a number of days to go. She hoped that the flower would be worth it. From what she had been told, there was only one place where the flower bloomed, and, if they were too late, they would miss it entirely. Jessica was not sure that she could wait another hundred years to see it or if she would be alive in another hundred years.

She clung into the back of her camel as they rode through the desert. The first day in the desert had been tough going, but she was tolerating it more. There was sand as far as the eye could see, and it was hot. Really hot.

She pulled her scarf up over her head as the sun rose to its highest point. It would not protect from the rays of the sun, but it did protect her skin from burning.

"What do you think the flower is going to be like?" she asked her mother.

"I think that it is going to be the most colorful flower in the world," replied her mother. "I think that it will be a rainbow of colors, or maybe a color that has not yet been discovered. It could be a color that no one can ever imagine in their wildest dreams. No matter what, it is going to be beautiful."

"I hope so," said Jessica.

The next day, the desert ended, and they scaled a mountain. It was a giant mountain, and undiscovered one, and much taller than Mount Everest. They slammed pickaxes into the smooth rock and drove hooks into the rock face to attach ropes to. It was hazardous, and they had to camp on the side of the mountain.

"Are you excited to see this flower?" asked Jessica.

"Oh, yes," replied her younger brother, who was happy to be climbing a mountain. "I think that it is going to be the biggest flower that we have ever seen. It might be so big that you can't see all of it at once. We might have to spend days looking at it. I heard that it is inside a volcano. Isn't that cool?"

"Yeah, pretty cool," said Jessica. "I hope that you are right about the flower. It would be pretty funny, though, if the flower was tiny."

"I guess," said her brother, and Jessica could tell that he did not think that would be funny.

After getting to the top of the ice-capped mountain, they started down the other side. It was almost as difficult to scale down as it was to scale up. The mountain was completely smooth, so they could slide down, but they had to use their axes to dig into the mountain as they did, or they would go too fast.

It took seven hours to slide down the mountain, and they camped at the bottom before they navigated through the swamp the next day. It was nice to sit by the fire after two days of climbing up and down the mountain, and they all sang songs as the fire crackled.

In the morning, they set off through the swamp. It bubbled up around them, and noxious gas came out. Jessica thought about throwing up a few times, but she managed to save herself from doing so.

They had to walk through the swamp as there was no way to go around it. The mud under the water stuck to the bottom of their boots, and they had to really pull up their feet to move forward. Each time they took a step, they would hear a big squelch.

There was the smell too. It was awful, like stinky cheese that has been left in the toilet.

"What do you think the flower will smell like?" asked Jessica, trying to take her mind off of the smell.

"It will smell terrific," said her uncle. He twisted his mustache, getting mud all over it. "I do not think that it will smell like anything that we have smelled before. You might not understand this, but I think that it will smell like my childhood."

"I understand," said Jessica. She did not understand, but it made her uncle smile, and she was happy about that. Jessica hoped that it didn't smell like her childhood. Her childhood smelled like a rotten swamp. She presumed that her uncle had never squelched through a rotten swamp as a child.

When they finally got out of the swamp, they washed up as best they could, and camped at the bottom of the volcano. The flower was inside.

"We have to time it right," said her father. "The flower will only bloom when the moon is full. Also, there is a 79% chance that the volcano will erupt tomorrow."

They all went to sleep, hoping that the volcano would not erupt while they were in their tents. Thankfully, it did not, though it was making a lot of noise when they got up in the morning, and it was threatening to erupt.

Once more, they scaled the side of a mountain, though this one was also a volcano. When they got to the top, they all looked in at the molten lava below. They waited for the moon to start to rise as the lava bubbled and became more heated. They all crossed their fingers that it would not erupt when they were inside of it.

When the moon was almost full, they attached the ropes to the mouth of the volcano and headed for the small spot of green below. They could not see from the top how big it was.

When they got to it, they could see that it was the same size as a dollar, but round instead of flat.

"Are you sure that this is it?" asked Jessica's uncle.

"This is definitely it," said her father. "We just have to wait for it to bloom. It is going to be spectacular."
The moonlight slowly made its way into the bubbling volcano and, when it hit the green bulb, the flower began to bloom. It shed the green and showed all of its glory.

The flower was very small, almost so small that you could not see it. It was also devoid of all color. It was a dull grey that could not be duller if it tied. Jessica's uncle leaned in close and smelled it.

"There is no smell," he said.

The entire family looked at the flower, a once in a lifetime opportunity, and then looked at each other.

"Shall we go home?" asked her father.

"Yes," said everyone.

The Labyrinth

Rocco looked into the labyrinth. The entrance was boring, but he knew that the labyrinth held many secrets.

He also knew the difference between a labyrinth and a maze. A Maze had an entrance and an exit. The goal of a maze was to get from the entrance to the exit. A labyrinth had one entrance and no exit. The goal of a labyrinth was to get to the center of the labyrinth and find whatever was there, usually treasure.

It had been a right of passage for everyone in his village to go into the labyrinth and get to the center. Only then would you truly be a Minotaurus. Rocco was sure that this meant there was a Minotaur somewhere in the labyrinth. A Minotaur is a beast that is half-bull and half-human. The bottom half is a bull, and the top half is human.

"Do you know," said Rocco to the guard on the gate, "that if you are ever lost in a maze, you can place your right hand on the wall and keep your hand on the wall, following the maze until you get to an entrance or an exit. It works every time."

"Hey, quit stalling," said the guard. "Either enter the labyrinth or…hey, I didn't know that. It really works?"

"Every time," said Rocco.

"Well, I'll be," said the guard. "Now, get in there." He gave Rocco a kick, sending him into the labyrinth.

Rocco had studied for this. Studied and trained.

His studying had told him that there was a test somewhere in the labyrinth. He did not know what to expect, but he knew that it was something that would help to make him into a better person.

His training had told him that there might be some danger. He had learned to use his agility to jump large distances, he could run really far, he was also fast. They had done a lot of sprint training, so there would definitely be something to run away from.

Will I have to run from the Minotaur, wondered Rocco.
He knew that Minotaurs were strong and fast, but there were also clever. And, while the top half was human, they did have horns on their heads. The threat of a horn sticking into his bum was enough motivation to run as fast as he could.

He was so lost in thought that he almost fell into the pit. He swung his arms as he almost stepped over the edge, just keeping his balance. At the bottom of the pit was a small pond of foul-smelling goo. It looked so sticky that he was not sure that he would get out.

Rocco took a few steps back and ran towards the pit. When he got to the edge, he stepped to the side and ran along the wall, using his speed to propel himself forward. He dived and rolled at the other side, landing perfectly.

"I need to pay more attention," he said to himself.

He did pay more attention, and his studying paid off. When he found a wall full of words, he could translate them all. They were in the old languages; Latin, Greek, Viking runes. They all said the same thing. They all said, 'Duck!'

Rocco was sure that they were not talking about the semi-aquatic animal, and he almost laughed to himself at the thought of ducks attacking. He was so caught up in his own little world that he almost forgot to duck.

A large cushion, attached to a massive chain, swung through the air like a giant pendulum. Rocco's reflexes kicked in, and he was able to duck just in time. The pillow would have thrown him across the labyrinth.

"Pillows are soft," Rocco said to no one. "They certainly are soft, but I have been in my fair share of pillow fights to know ho much they can hurt when they whack you in the head."

Rocco continued on but vowed to take the labyrinth more seriously. Twice, he had almost fell victim to a trap through his own foolishness.

"Let's do this," said Rocco.

After walking for twenty minutes, he started to feel hungry. He could not believe his eyes when he saw a table packed with cakes and candy. The pile was so high that he was sure people would be able to see it from outside of the labyrinth.

There was also a sign in the table that read:

Please eat the cake and candy. They are definitely not poisoned, and in no way will they send you to sleep for two days. Completely normal candy and cakes, oh yes, yes sir, nothing suspect here, just go ahead and eat them.

Rocco decided not to eat anything, which was a good decision as they were all filled with sleeping powder. If he had eaten anything, he would have been put to sleep for two days.

Rocco felt hungry as he walked through the labyrinth, but he was too strong to give in. He knew that once he left the labyrinth, he would have a large feast waiting for him. His older sister had made it through the labyrinth, his mother and father also. All of his grandparents had made it through, and he was going to make it through too.

"Where are you, Minotaur?" asked Rocco. For a brief moment, he felt brave, even though he had nothing to protect himself with.

That moment disappeared when he reached the center of the labyrinth. There, in the middle of the labyrinth, was the Minotaur. He stood, staring at Rocco. Rocco could see that there was nothing else there, no treasure, nothing. Just the Minotaur.

There was an assortment of weapons on the wall to his left and the wall to his right. Rocco was afraid. The Minotaur was bigger than anything he had ever seen before, and muscular too. He did not think that he could defeat the beast.

He looked the Minotaur in the eyes, and looked back to the weapons, checking each one. There were swords, axes, shields, maces, and every other weapon you could imagine. Rocco looked back at the Minotaur and made his choice.

Rocco walked forward empty-handed.

"Welcome, Rocco," said the Minotaur. He bowed to Rocco.

"Thank you," said Rocco as he bowed back.

"Why did you not attack me?" asked the Minotaur.

"I didn't want to," replied Rocco. "You have never done me any harm, and I have come into your labyrinth unannounced. Why should I harm you? I was scared of you because I have never seen you before, but that is no reason to attack. When I thought about it, I decided that it would be better to meet you. I should not be scared of you because you are different."

"You are wise, Rocco," said the Minotaur. "Your wisdom will serve you well in the world. It is a pleasure to meet you, and you may come back any time to talk with me, but, for now, you must go."

"Why?" asked Rocco. "Is it dangerous here."

"Not at all," said the Minotaur. "Your feast and your family are waiting, and you must be famished."

Rocco had to admit that he was very hungry. He said goodbye to the Minotaur and left the labyrinth through the secret tunnel. His family was waiting for him, and they all gave him big hugs. They also had a feast waiting, and Rocco had never enjoyed his food more than he did after escaping the labyrinth.

The Story Of Sleep

Once upon a time, a long, long time ago, there was no sleep.

Can you imagine that? There was no sleep in the entire world.

When night came, people continued to do what they did during the day. Some people worked, others played, and some spent time with their families. But, most found that they daydreamed. They would sit during the night and daydream. When they did, they all felt a little better.

But, for the most part, people felt bad. There was something missing from their lives, and they did not know what.

It was the king who finally helped to solve the problem, though not for the reasons that you might think. He was bored with nighttime. All of the cool things happened during the day, and it was always dark at night. It was harder to play sports, people daydreamed a lot (or should that be night dreamed?), and people always seemed to be busy.

The king wished for it to be day all of the time.

So, he went to his scientists.

"When the sun goes down, the day is done," said the king. "I want you to stop the sun from going down so that it can be day all of the time, then the fun will never end."

The scientists went to work. They had many ideas, as many scientists do, and set to work trying to keep the sun in the sky for longer.

They tried to create a big net to catch the sun, but could not create one that was big enough. The tried to build a tower under the sun to stop it from moving, but could not get planning permission. They even tried asking the sun to stop moving, but the sun did not listen to them.

When they went back to the king, they told him, "We cannot stop the sun from moving."

"Hmm," said the king. "Well, if you cannot stop the day from leaving, can we time travel?"

"What do you mean?" asked the scientists.

"What if you create a machine that time travels to the future? When the moon rises, we can jump into the time machine and travel to the future, when the sun is rising again. That way, we can skip the night altogether."

"An interesting idea," said the scientists. They set to work building a time machine but found that it was impossible to do, and they could only make time *seem* to move faster. They found that when they were doing something fun, it felt like time was moving faster. And, when they were doing something boring, it felt like time slowed down.

But, no matter what they did, they could not travel through time.

"What about a fake sun?" asked the king. "We could pretend that it is still day by shining a big light over the world, and then it would be day all the time."

So, the scientists got back to work.

They built the biggest light that people had ever seen and shone it over the world. At night, it was turned on, and during the day, it was switched off. And, for a brief time, the king was happy.

For a time, everyone was happy. But, they found that it was harder to daydream. They also found that everything became more difficult. They felt more and more tired. Still, the King continued to shine the light, thinking that he was doing something good for his kingdom.

A knock soon came at the castle door, and three wise men were shown into the castle. They met with the king.

"You have created an imbalance," said the wise man of the body.

"You cannot un-split day and night," said the wise man of the mind.

"We will teach you our secrets," said the wise man of emotions.

"Your secrets," said the king.

"You were misinformed," said the wise man of the mind. "Time travel is possible, but not the way in which you think. We are here to teach you how to time travel through the night so that you can do as much as you can through the day."

"By resting," said the wise man of emotions, "you can function better."

"Teach me, teach me," said the king.

So, the three wise men taught the king all that they knew.

"First, you must rest your body," said the wise man of the body. "This is the easiest part, but you must practice it a lot."

The wise man of the body instructed the king in what he needed to do. He showed the king how to lie on a comfortable surface, and let go of all the tension in his body. The king did what the wise man said, filling a large bag with hay, and lying on top of it.

For a week, the king did this, lying perfectly still for eight hours every night, until he could do it without moving his body. On the seventh night, he found that his body would sometimes move by itself. He also felt very rested after seven nights, though he was very bored too. It is hard to lay still when you cannot do anything.

"Good," said the wise man of the body. "You have mastered the first step."

"Now, you must master the next," said the wise man of the mind. "For seven more nights, you must do the same, but you must clear your mind."

The wise man of the mind instructed the king on how to empty his mind of everything. The king tried as hard as he could. Every night, he got onto his hay pile, did not move his body, and tried to empty his mind.

As the week went on, he got better and better. On the first night, he could not help but think how silly this all was. On the third night, he thought about everything he wanted to be doing. On the fifth night, he thought about what he wanted to do with his life. And, on the seventh night, he thought about nothing. His mind was completely blank.

"Good," said the wise man of the mind.

"But I felt so bored," admitted the king.

"That is where I come in," said the wise man of emotion. "Now, you must learn the final step in this process."

"Teach me," said the king. He had to admit that he had never felt more rested.

"You must do the same as before. You must let your body rest, and you must let your mind empty of thought, but you must also hold onto any emotions that you have had throughout your day. When you hold these emotions in your mind, do not think of what happened, think about the feeling."

The king did as he was instructed. This was the hardest part of the process.

For the first few nights, he thought about the good things that had happened and could see them in his mind. He also thought of the bad things and lived them over and over. He felt angry.

On the fifth night, he could feel all the emotions well, but he could still picture the incidents in his mind. He saw them from different angles, watching himself in the images.

On the seventh night, he finally let go. He held the emotion in his body, but he did not hold the pictures in his mind.

On the seventh night, he finally dreamed.

"That was amazing," said the king when he woke up the next day. "I feel so rested."

"We have taught you our secrets," said the three wise men. "It is now time for us to go. You must teach everyone to travel through the night."

The king agreed, and he taught everyone how to sleep and dream.

From Red To Green

Sometimes it is hard to move from red to green. Have you ever tried? Do you even know what I am talking about?

Red is when you are angry. If you are angry and annoyed about something, if you have so much pent up frustration that you think that you are going to explode, then you are in the red zone.

It is easy to get into the red zone, and it can be tricky to get out of it. You do not even have to do anything to get into it, and it can take over your mind.

Almost anything can get you into the red zone. Maybe you did not get to do what you wanted to do today. Perhaps you played a game and had no luck at all. Did you fall over when you were playing sport and missed scoring a point for your team?

Lots of things can get you into the red zone, and that is okay because I'll tell you a little secret. Adults get into the red zone all of the time. The trick is to get out of the red zone. Once you know how to get out of the red zone, you can do it all of the time, and you can even teach adults to do it.

But, it does take a lot of practice.

So, if you want to get out of the red zone, where do you go?

You go to the green zone.

But what is the green zone?

The green zone is the place where you are calm and happy. You are not angry there. You are peaceful and serene. It is the exact opposite of the red zone.

It is the feeling that you have when you are just falling asleep and do not have a care in the world. It is like having a warm blanket wrapped around you, or a hug from your family. It is the feeling you get when you watch the ocean waves lapping on the beach, or listen to the sound of a river.

When you are in the green zone, you are happy and calm.

Wouldn't you like to be in the green zone instead of the red zone?

Sometimes it is not so easy. When you are in the red zone, it is hard to leave. When you are in the red zone, sometimes you do not want to leave. Sometimes you want to stay there forever.

That is why you have to practice getting out of the red zone before you even get there. When you practice it over and over, you will be able to get out of the red zone easily when you are there.

So, what can you do?

Here are some exercises to practice to get from the red zone to the green zone. The more that you practice them, the better you will get. Let's practice some of them now.

First, we are going to squeeze some lemons. Why lemons? I don't really know, by they are as good a thing as any. Of course, we are not using real lemons. We are using imaginary lemons.

So, close your eyes and imagine that you have lemons in your hands, one in each. They are slightly cool to touch, and they have bumpy skin. Hold one in each hand, and start to squeeze them.

When you are doing this, actually tense your hands and pretend that you are squeezing real lemons. Feel the skin tearing and the juice coming out. If you destroy these ones, move onto some more lemons and squeeze them too. Squeeze as many lemons as you like, or until you start to feel more green than red.

Now, when you get into the red zone, you can squeeze lemons to get you back to the green zone.

Our second method is to have an angry dance party.

You might not want to do this now if you are calmly in bed, but you can practice it in the morning if you like. All you are going to do is to put on some music, a little louder than usual, and dance to it.

Now, you want something with a little bit of a beat to it so you can dance quickly and angrily. You do not want to damage anything or anyone, so make sure that there is nothing in the way if you want to flail your arms around.

Dance for as long as you can. Dance quickly and angrily. When you are having your angry dance party, try to use the same songs too. This will help you when you are in the red zone.

So, when you do get into the red zone, you can switch on that music and start dancing to it. When you are tired out, flop down on the couch or your bed and get your breath back.

The next tool that you will use is writing and drawing, and you do not need to be any good at either to do this. All you have to do is try, and you will help yourself to feel better. Moving from red to green is a much more valuable skill than drawing pretty pictures, though that is fun too.

For this exercise, find a piece of paper and a pencil or pen. You are going to write down exactly how you feel. If you do not feel angry right now, think about a time that you were, and write down how you felt. If you are not yet great at printing on paper, or if you do not want to, you can draw how you feel.

When you draw, you do not need to draw a picture if you do not want to. You can draw a color that shows how you feel or scribbles that represent your anger. Draw exactly how you feel without thinking about it.

When you are done writing or drawing, you can show a parent or guardian if you want. If you want to talk about it, you can. If you do not want to talk about it, you do not have to.

If you are still feeling angry after writing or drawing, then tear up the paper. Go ahead, rip it into as many pieces as you want and throw it up in the air (make sure to clean up when you are back in the green zone).

When you get into the red zone, pull out some paper and pencils, and show how you are feeling.

These tools take time and practice to master. That is why you need to practice them when you are in the green zone, and you are calm and happy.

The more you practice, the more you will be able to do them when you are in the red zone. Do not worry if you cannot do them every time, the red zone is a tough place to be, but the more you try, the more it will happen.

The red zone is not a bad place, it is just a place where our emotions are, and that makes us who we are. Everyone gets angry, even those people in your family. Once you can master the red zone, you will become a better person.

For now, it is time to sleep (unless you are reading this during the day. If you are, then now is the time to practice).

Well done for listening to or reading this story. It is the first step in your journey from the red zone to the green zone, and your first step to becoming a better person.

The Wind

The wind can come in many forms. Sometimes it comes to us in tiny little wisps that blow through our hair, lifting it slightly. Those tiny zephyrs of air like to play with the leaves in the trees, or stir up those on the ground.

Sometimes, the wind blows a little harder. That kind of wind is amazing when you are riding your bike or playing soccer. It helps to cool you, especially when you are really sweaty. This is the kind of wind that likes to lift plastic bags from the garbage and toss them in the air, making them dance.

Then, there is the wind that is a little louder. This wind can be hard to walk through. When it comes at night, it can make funny noises as it rushes past your home, noises like an elephant trumping or a witch whistling.

The last type of wind is the wind that you do not want to be caught in. It can swirl in large circles and lift houses from the ground. Thankfully, that wind does not come very often.

The wind can be gentle, and it can be tough, just like you. The wind also likes to travel. Every day, the wind travels around the entire world. It sees so many amazing people and things. Every day, it visits you. The wind thinks that you are pretty amazing.

What does the wind see as it travels around the world?

There are too many amazing things to count, but here are some of them.

Though the wind cannot get underwater very easily, it can stir up the water. When the wind travels over Australia, it likes to stay still and calm the water so that it can see the Great Barrier Reef.

The Great Barrier Reef is underwater and is a living thing. It is made out of coral and houses lots of different animals. Lots of fish live there, along with dolphins and whales. It stretches for more than 3,000 kilometers. That might be even bigger than the country that you live in. There are even turtles and sea snakes that live there.

The Great Wall of China is another place that the wind likes to blow over. The wall is strong, so the wind does not have to worry about being calm. Did you know that the Great Wall of China was built over 2,000 years ago? That is a very long time ago.

When it was built, it was created to stop people from invading and attacking. Thankfully, there are no attackers anymore, and people can even walk on top of the wall. Yes, it is wide enough to walk on top of it!

In India, there is a beautiful palace. It is called the Taj Mahal. It is one of the most beautiful buildings in the world, and the wind can blow all around without damaging it. It was created as a present from a man to a woman. He built it to show how much he loved her.

When the wind gets to America, it heads straight for the Grand Canyon. It is fun to blow over the land, and move across dusty plains or up mountains, but you can make really cool noises if you blow through crevices or valleys. The Grand Canyon has lots of valleys.

If you were to try and hike through the Grand Canyon, it would take you a lot of time to get from one end to the other. The valleys are deep, and there are rivers that run through it. It can also get really hot. But, that is no problem for the wind, and it likes to go there to play.

There are many waterfalls in the world, and the one that the wind likes best is the Iguaza falls in Brazil and Argentina. If you have ever seen a waterfall, then you know how cool they can be, but I bet that you have never seen a waterfall that is as big as this!

The waterfall is so loud that you might not even be able to hear the wind when you are there. The wind likes to go there, even if it cannot be heard sometimes. The thing it likes most about going to Iguaza falls is making the water dance. As the water falls, it is fun to blow it across the sky.

The Sagrada Familia in Spain is a building like no other that you will ever see, and the wind likes to go there and perch in the trees beside it. Sometimes the wind will just sit there and take in the beauty of the building. The building is known as a Basilica and was designed by a famous artist, Antoni Gaudi. He never got to finish it, and people are still building parts of it today, even though it was started over a hundred years ago.

The Scottish Highlands are an amazing place to go if you want some peace and quiet, as long as you don't mind the sound of sheep and, of course, and the wind. The wind loves to go there, and I know this because the Scottish Highlands can be a very windy place.

They are beautiful too. There are large stony mountains, rolling green hills, purple heather, thistles, and lots of animals. The wind likes to tickle the fur and hair of the animals. There are stags, sheep, highland cows, otters, beavers, mice, birds, and more. If you are very sneaky, you might even see a haggis running around too. The wind has seen one, or so it tells me.

The wind also likes to visit the places where no people live, like deserted islands and places where it is very cold. Of course, some people live in the cold, but most do not. The wind visits all of the places where there are only animals.

There are some islands where only penguins live, or where seals hunt, or where walruses bask, or where dolphins and whales swim. Sometimes there are sea lions, and giant tortoises, and marine iguanas, and wonderful birds and fish. The wind loves every living being on earth.

The wind also goes to Mount Everest and sits on top of the world. From up there, it can see everything, and it can blow as hard as it wants without damaging anything. Of course, sometimes there are visitors at the top of Mount Everest, and the wind tries not to blow so hard, but it gets excited often and cannot help it.

The deserts are also fun to visit. There are not usually too many people there, so it can blow as hard as it wants, and sand is very fun to blow around. Have you ever played with sand? It is fun, right? The wind likes to blow it around and create shapes. There are lots of sand dunes in the desert, large piles of sand, and that is all created by the wind.

Blowing all day is hard work, so sometimes, the wind does not blow at all. When it has a lot of energy, it will blow a lot and, when it is tired, it will stop. If you were the wind, where would you travel to, and who would you visit?

It is hard work being the wind. There is always something to do and somewhere to go. The wind is always traveling, seeing everything and everyone that the world has to offer, and that includes you.

So, the next time that you feel the wind on your face, or your hair is lifted, or a breeze ruffles your clothes, know that it is the wind just come to visit. If you have the time, make sure to wave to the wind and say hello.

When The Moon Disappeared

Luna perched on the top of the craggy rock, looking down below. There had been some talk of wolves in the area, and she was there to make sure that they did not get too close to her village. She was the head of the elf scouts and always made sure that the rest of the elves in her village were taken care of.

"Something feels weird," she said to Barko.

Barko was her second in command and the nicest elf that anyone had ever met. But, you would not know that to look at him. He stood almost a foot taller than any other elf and had a scar on his cheek. He had got that scar when he fell off his bike as a child, but everyone thought that he got it in battle.

While Luna was not as tall as Barko, she was just as fierce. She could use her words to get things done, and she was the smartest elf in the village. That was why she was the leader of the elf scours and tasked with protecting the village.

"What do you think it is?" asked Barko.

"I don't know," said Luna. "Just feels off, like something is about to happen."

They looked to the distance and could see wolves there, but the wolves were running away from the village. Luna did not think that her village was under any danger, but she was still wary. She tugged on her pointy ears, as she always did when she was deep in thought, and whistled an elven tune.

"What did the village elder say?" asked Luna.

"Only that hard times were coming. That the wolves and the water would be affected," replied Barko.

"The wolves and the water. What could that be? Maybe she was wrong," suggested Luna, touching the arrows on her back. She was an amazing shot with her bow and arrow.

"She's never been wrong before," said Barko.

"That's true," responded Luna.

They descended into silence, listening only to the sound of the crickets chirping in the darkness. Luna looked all around her, everything beautiful and basked in moonlight. She tried to think about what could affect the wolves and the water.

Her eyes widened in surprise as it came to her, though she was still skeptical about the entire thing. She suddenly looked up, and Barko looked up to. They both stared at the moon.

"The moon," they said together.

As they said it, almost as if they had triggered the event, the moon began slowly shrinking. It got smaller and smaller until it was only a dot in the sky, and then it disappeared.

Luna and Barko looked at each other. This was a serious issue, and it had to be fixed, but they did not know how. There was nothing to do right now, so they returned to their village and slept.

In the morning, they told everyone what they had seen. A village meeting was called, but no one knew what to do about it. Even the village elders had to think more about the issue. Luna decided to talk to the ones who might know something.

"Come on, Barko," she said. "We have some investigating to do.

They made the trip through the forest and across the plains until they came to the ocean. When they got there, they could see that the ocean had been crying. It was sitting where it normally sat, but it was not moving. The ocean was depressed.

"Oh, Great Ocean," said Luna. "We have come for your help. The moon has disappeared, and we do not know what to do."

"You do not know what to do!" boomed the ocean. "Look at me! What am I going to do?"

"Can we help?" asked Luna.

"No one can help me," said the ocean. "My tides have gone. I always worked in harmony with the moon, my tides would ebb and flow. It would make me happy, the beach would be happy, the sea creatures would be happy, and everyone else would be happy."

"I have found a lot of joy watching your waves and tides," said Barko. "I always came here as a young boy."

"Well, now that is gone," said the ocean. "The moon is gone forever."

"Is it really gone?" asked Luna.

"I think so," said the ocean. "I can still remember the moon, but it is like a distant memory. I cannot help you."

Luna and Barko left the ocean to be sad. They did not know what they could do to help it, but they had to try. They went to visit the wolves next.

The elves and the wolves had never been friends, but there had always been a respect between them. When Luna and Barko got close to the wolf village, they expected some warning growls, but there were none. When they entered the village, the wolves were lazing around, lying on the ground.

"What happened?" asked Luna.

"There is no point to anything anymore," said a wolf.

"What do you mean?" asked Luna.

"If there is no moon to howl at, then what point in life is there. We have always howled at the moon, but not the moon is gone," said the wolf.

"Can you not howl at something else?" asked Barko.

"How dare you!" growled the wolf. "We cannot go around just howling at anything. We have howled at the moon for centuries. We're not animals!"

The wolf walked off.

"I hope that it returns," muttered an old wolf who was standing close to them.

"What do you mean?" asked Luna.

"Please, just leave us," said the old wolf. "We are in too much pain to have this stirred up."

Luna and Barko agreed to leave, but something was stirring inside of Luna. When she got back to the village, she shared her finings with the other elves.

"I have a feeling that the moon is gone, but not forgotten. I think that it is still out there, and the ocean and wolves can still feel it," said Luna.

"Hmm," said an elder. "Then we may be able to bring it back."

"We have been studying the old texts," said another of the elders. "It seems that the moon would often travel when it did not feel needed anymore. It would only come back after a number of years, but we can perform the moon dance to bring it back. If we show the moon that it is loved, we can bring it back."

"What do we need to do?" asked Luna.

The preparations were made, and everyone in the village was outside as the night fell. Without the moon, there was not as much light as there used to be, and large fires had to be lit.

The elders gave out the instructions.

As large drums were beaten, the elves gathered in large circles, dancing with hands linked, around and around in the shape of the moon.

They broke hands and held their arms out, waving them from side to side like the tides. A strange wind blew over the village, and Luna was sure that she could hear the ocean's sound. She was convinced that the ocean was dancing too.

When the water part was done, everyone shook their bodies and took in a large breath of air. Still shaking their bodies, they let out a large howl, pointing it upwards towards the sky. One, two, three times they did it, but nothing happened.

Then, there was another howl. The wolves had joined in, howling for the moon to return. As the wolves howled, the ocean moved, and the people danced, the moon could see how much it was missed, and returned to shine on the world.

Every year after that, on the same day the moon first disappeared, the elves all gathered to dance the dance of the moon. The ocean and the wolves joined in too, and the moon never disappeared again.

The Luckiest Boy In The World

John did not know it when he was born, but he was destined to become the luckiest boy in the world.

Even the story of his birth is quite lucky. His parents were hiking in Peru, halfway up a mountain, hundreds of miles away from any other people, and a great distance from any hospitals when John decided it was time to be born.

Now, you might be thinking that it was a silly decision to go hiking so far from anywhere when you are pregnant, and you would be right, but John's mom and dad were searching for a lost city, and it was still a week before he was due to be born, so they did not think that anything bad would happen.

They were wrong.

Just as they discovered a building from the lost village, only the second time it had ever been discovered in history, John's mom started to give birth.

This would have been a big problem if John was not so lucky.

As his parents ran into the building to find somewhere soft to rest, they discovered some doctors and nurses who just happened to be taking a vacation with all of their medical equipment (they were the first people in history to discover this lost village).

"Well, this is certainly lucky," said the doctor, who had, for some reason, just washed and sanitized her hands in case she was needed.

"Yes," said the nurses, who had only just finished setting up a comfortable bed in case someone would need it.

The birth went without a hitch. There was even lots of green clover around, which was even luckier, especially as it was not supposed to grow there.

As John grew up, he got luckier and luckier.

There was one time, and one time only, that he was bullied. Well, someone tried to bully him, but they never tried again.
John was standing beside a stream, and an older boy walked past, thinking that it would be funny to kick John in. John was facing the water, so he did not see the kick coming, but he did move out of the way just in time, distracted by a rare silver and pink butterfly. The older boy splashed straight into the stream.

Well, the older boy was so annoyed that he decided to give John a wedgie. He ran after John, trying to pull John's underwear up at the back so that it would really hurt, and John was too busy not walking under a ladder to notice this older boy.

Through some strange turn of events, that I won't even try to describe here because they are too indescribable, the older boy managed to give himself a wedgie, kick himself in the shin, and then hang himself in a tree.

When John finally turned around, he saw the boy hanging in the tree and helped him down. The older boy was very grateful, and John was never bullied from that day. Not that anyone would be able to if they tried.

There was also the big soccer game. His school team was in the final of the biggest tournament in the country. They were not the best team, but they did have a lot of luck. John's team was trailing by two goals with only one minute to go.

The other team was attacking, and, for some reason, John decided to kick the ball towards his own goal. The goalkeeper dived for the ball and missed it. The ball hit the post and rebounded all the way to the other end of the field, going straight into the other goal. The other goalkeeper had been paying so little attention that he did not even notice the ball trickle past him.

He paid more attention when the game restarted with forty seconds to go, but could not stop the ball the next time. The other team kicked off and booted the ball. It somehow hit John's bum, flew up the field, and looped over the goalkeeper. He could do nothing to stop it.

When the game kicked off again with ten seconds to go, the other team tried to hold onto the ball but, through events that are not even worth describing, the ball ended up in their goal again through sheer luck. John's team had won.

Don't even get me started on the time he managed to score two baskets at the same time with one ball in basketball or how he managed to score nine home runs with one hit in baseball.

Any game that John plays, he wins, so do not play games with him. There are also some games that he was won by not playing. There was a marathon too. He ran away from an angry dog one time and ended up running an entire marathon, winning it by more than seven minutes.

When he was five, he got into a bike accident and almost joined the circus. He was riding his bike in a field, close to a place where there was a circus, but he had no idea of this. He rode his bike quickly down a hill, and, when he hit the bottom, his wheel got stuck in a hole, and he went flying over the handlebars.

He would have hit the ground it someone had not left a trampoline in the exact spot that he was due to land. After bouncing on the trampoline, he landed in a circus canon. That cushioned his fall, and everything would have been fine if it had not been for his momentum.

The cannon was pointing away from the circus tent. Still, the momentum shifted the cannon so that it pointed directly toward the tent. A small campfire that had just been lit, and unattended for exactly nine seconds, lit the cannon fuse and sent John flying through the air again.

He thought that he was done for this time as he headed toward the large canvas tent. The wind blew and opened a small slit in the tent, where the stitches had come away. It was just big enough for John to fit through.

If the trapeze artist had jumped at the right time, there would be no one to catch John, but she had felt her lace come undone and bent down to tie it. That was when John flew over her shoulder and across the circus tent. The man on the other trapeze caught him, and he looked as surprised as John did.

The crowd went wild, and John was offered a job in the circus. He declined. He was only five, and he would much rather go to school. School would be much more fun than the circus. And it was. John got up to so many fun and lucky things in school that I would have to write an entire book just to describe them.

One of those things included becoming a teacher for the day, and the other included saving the school from dinosaurs, but you probably don't want to hear about that.

Anyway, what would you do if you were as lucky as John? If you could drink a magic potion or have a magic spell cast on you, and you would become the luckiest person in the world for one day, what would you do?

I hope that, as you go to sleep tonight, you dream of all the things that you would do.

Goodnight.

Survival

"I'm going out," said Amy.

"Have fun," said her parents.

Amy was only eight years old, but she was independent and feisty. She loved to learn new things, and always wanted to learn new skills. One of her favorite things to do was to go outside with her friends and pretend that they were camping out in an inhospitable climate.

An inhospitable climate is a place where it is difficult to live. When you live in a place like that, you have to do all that you can to survive.

Amy's friends were all busy today, so she headed off into the small woods by herself. She could have lots of fun on her own.

She had her bag with her, and, in that bag, she had packed all of the essentials. She had some string, a flashlight, a warm hat, flint and steel, her stuffed bunny, Hopsy, two granola bars, an apple, some water, a small knife, and zip ties. It was all she would need should she be lost in an inhospitable environment.

As Amy walked into the woods, she got completely lost. She had been in the woods many times before, and she had never got lost, but this time she did.

"Okay, I have to survey my surroundings," she said.

She was good at survival, and she knew that she had to get the lie of the land before she did any planning. She found a good climbing tree, one with lots of branches, and climbed to the top. When she got there, she checked all around her.

On one side, there was an ocean, mountains were on another, the forest stretched as far as she could see in another direction, and a swamp made up the rest. She even brought Hopsy from the bag to confirm what she saw. He confirmed it with a nod.

She was sleepy by this time, so she thought it best to make a shelter where she could sleep. At the base of the tree, she gathered thick branches and placed them up against it. After that, she placed smaller branches and leaves on top, finishing it off with moss.

It was a very nice shelter, and she placed Hopsy in it to look after it while she went off in search of food. She found some berries close by and came back to camp. When she returned, she took the flint and steel from her bag. She could use them to make some fire.

She gathered some large logs, put small ones on top, and topped that with dry leaves and kindling. She used the flint and steel to make a spark. There was soon a roaring fire. Amy and Hopsy ate berries while the fire crackled.

When she was a little more tired, Amy retreated to the enclosure. Hopsy stayed by the fire to keep a lookout. When Amy woke, the fire had gone out, and Hopsy was fast asleep.

"Great lookout, you are," she said to Hopsy, nudging him with her foot.

Amy had thought that someone might come looking for her, but they had not. They would have to spend more time in the wilderness.

"More food," said Amy as her stomach rumbled.

There was only one thing to do. She would have to build a raft and go fishing in the ocean. She packed up her stuff and walked to the shore. When she got there, she found some nice logs and bound them together with string and zip ties to make a raft.

She found a piece of wire and bent it into a hook, tying some string to it. All she needed now was some bait. Digging a big hole helped her to discover lots of worms. She put one worm on the hook and ate one, popping it in her mouth and chewing on it. She was really hungry. Hopsy ate one too.

She pushed the raft out, hopped on, and dropped the hook into the water. It did not take long for her to catch a rainbow fish, catfish, and flying fish. Back at the shore, she started another fire, and she and Hopsy ate the fish while looking out over the waves.

"We need to find our way home, Hopsy," said Amy. She did not think that anyone was out looking for her. "Animals are smart, we should follow one."

Amy was very good at tracking animals, especially rabbits. Hopsy was a rabbit, and she had spent a lot of time with him. She did not find any rabbit tracks, but she did find a deer track and possibly a coyote footprint.

She followed the deer prints through the forest. They took her away from the ocean and deeper into the trees. When she came out on the other side, there were no deers, but there were penguins. They were all very cute.

Amy was glad that she had packed her warm hat and put it on before she froze. She took a sip from her bottle of water, saving some for later. It was always wise to ration food and water, and that was why she had not eaten her granola bars yet.

"Do you know the way to go, penguins?" asked Amy.

The penguins honked at her, but she did not speak penguin, so she had no idea what they were saying. She walked past them and continued up the snowbank, hoping to find a landmark that she would use. She had a vague idea of what her house looked like, and was sure that she would recognize it when she saw it.

When she got to the top of the snowbank, she only saw a desert beyond it. She thought that it was weird for a snow tundra and a desert to be side by side, but she decided not to question it, she had other things to worry about.

When she was in the desert, she thought about taking off the hat, but it was smarter to keep it on. It would make her hotter, but it would save her from burning. And, she had saved lots of water, so she was sure that she could make it through.

"Be brave," she said to Hopsy.

Some sand snakes soon appeared, but she tied them together with zip ties so that they could not bite her. Luckily, she found a camel soon after that, and the camel let her ride on its back. That helped her to get through the desert, and she was soon on the other side.

When she reached the volcano, she hoped that she was going the right way. She knew that she could not go back, so she scaled it instead. At the top, she found a cave full of treasure. There was gold, and diamonds, and other precious gems. There was also a dragon in there too.

The dragon would have got her if it were not for the flashlight. She pulled it out of her pocket and shined it on the treasure. Rays of light bounced off, blinding the dragon so that they could escape. Hopsy almost got bitten.
They ran down the other side of the volcano and tumbled into a forest.

"Hey, this looks familiar," said Amy.

They walked through the forest, and Amy found her back yard. She was home! She ran through her yard and into the house.

"I'm home!" she shouted.

"Welcome home," said her mother.

"Weren't you worried?" asked Amy. "I was gone for such a long time. It must have been days. There were penguins, dragons, a volcano, swamps, trees, oceans, rafts, fires, and adventure."

"That's fun," said her mother. "I'm glad that you played outside by yourself for so long. You were gone for over an hour."

Amy folded her arms and sighed. Adults were never very good at keeping time.

Amy went back upstairs and packed her sword and shield into her bag. Next time, she would slay the dragon and take its treasure.

The Angry Crocodile

Crocodile was an angry crocodile. No one was quite sure why Crocodile was such an angry crocodile, but they knew better than to hang around when he came walking along. He was always shouting and chomping, and the other animals were scared that they would have their heads bitten off.

Bear first met Crocodile when he was fishing. Bear sat on the banks of the river, dropping his fishing line into the water, hoping to catch some fish for his dinner. He had only been there for six minutes when Crocodile appeared. It was the first and last time that Bear met Crocodile.

The crocodile came waking out of the water, gnashing his teeth, and shouting things that Bear could not make out. Bear did not waste any time. He dropped his fishing rod, knocked over his small chair, scrambled up the bank, knocking over his snacks and drinks, and ran home as fast as he could.

Bear never went back to the river again.

Most animals ran away when they saw Crocodile, but Owl tried something different. He had studied animal brains his whole life, and he was sure that Crocodile was angry because of something that had happened in his past.

Owl kept a lookout for Crocodile, and, when he saw him walking about on the banks of the river, chomping his teeth, he made his move. Owl swooped from his tree, flew close to Crocodile, and alighted on a branch in a nearby tree.

"I am here to help you," said Owl.

"Roar!" shouted Crocodile.

"Tell me about your past," said Owl.

"I was walking," said Crocodile.

"No, no," said Owl. "Tell me about your parents. What were they like? How was your childhood?"

"Can you," started Crocodile.

"Has something happened to you?" asked Owl. "Something happened in your past, didn't it, and that is why you are so angry. Share your pain with me, Crocodile."

"I was walking," said Crocodile.

"Oh, well, if you are not going to help yourself, then I cannot help you," said Owl. He flew off back to his home, chasing his head and hooting.

The next animal to try and help Crocodile was Fox. Fox had watched Owl try to help Crocodile and was sure that he had failed because Crocodile had been so angry.

"There is no point in trying to talk with him when he is so angry," said Fox to himself. "Now, to prepare."

Fox found cleaning in the forest and made it as calming as possible. He found camomile flowers and lavender. He laid them out in the clearing, and they created the most amazing smell. Fox asked the bees for some honey, and he placed a bowl of honey in the middle of the clearing. That would surely help to calm him.

He found some candles, leftovers from a human camping trip, and placed them around the clearing, though he did not light them as fire is dangerous in the forest. He also found some insects to come and hum a nice song.

When all was ready, Fox went down to the banks of the river and shouted, "Crocodile, come here! I can help you!"

It did not take long for Crocodile to come blustering from the river. He raised his front foot and waved it in the air.

"Yeah, come and get me!" shouted Fox.

Crocodile took a few steps forward and waved his foot in the air again.

"Yeah, you are so angry!" shouted Fox. "Only a little bit more, and you can get rid of your anger."

Fox continued to shout at Crocodile, while Crocodile followed and shook his foot in the air. When Fox had finally lured Crocodile to the clearing, he stood back, relaxed, and watched the results of his hard work.

Crocodile immediately destroyed everything, stomping over all of the flowers, biting the candles, and scaring the insects away. He even stuck his foot in the honey instead of eating it.

"Well, I cannot help you," complained Fox. He trotted away, shaking his head.

Tiger stood and watched the whole thing. He laughed as Fox tried to calm the crocodile.

"He doesn't need to be calmed," said Tiger. "He needs someone to show him that he is not the only angry one. I will show him that he is not alone, and, if that does not work, I will show him just how angry I can be."

Tiger wasted no time and jumped out in front of Crocodile.

"Well, you think that you are angry? Look how angry I am!" shouted Tiger. He leaped around in a circle, moving around Crocodile, as the crocodile shook honey from his foot.

"I don't know what," Crocodile started shouting, but Tiger only shouted louder.

"I don't want to hear your excuses!" shouted Tiger. "Do you think that you are the only angry one in the world? I am angry too!"

"My foot!" shouted Crocodile.

"Yes, your foot is covered in honey!" shouted Tiger. "I don't care, you did that to yourself. You think that you can be angry for no reason!"

"My foot!" shouted Crocodile again.

"Oh, be quiet about your foot!" shouted Tiger. "You think that you are angry, well I am even angrier. When I get done showing you just how angry I can be, you will never want to be angry ever again!"

Tiger roared even louder, drowning out all of Crocodile's roars and words. Tiger bounded up and down, roaring and gnashing his teeth. He swiped at trees, stomped flowers, and scared away any other animals that dared to come close.

When Tiger was done, he was out of breath, but he was proud of himself because he had helped this silly crocodile. When Crocodile roared again, Tiger lost his smile. He thought that he had helped, but he had not.
"There is no helping you," said Tiger. "If you want to be angry, then go ahead. You can be the angriest animal in the entire world, for all that I care." Tiger bounded off and never returned.

Squirrel sat on the tree branch, eating an acorn. He had watched all of the animals in turn as they tried to help Crocodile. He took another bite of the nut and sighed.

"Crocodile!" he shouted.

The crocodile looked up at the tree and chomped his teeth.

"Has anyone actually asked you why you are angry?" asked Squirrel.

"I have tried to tell them," shouted Crocodile. "I tried to ask Bear for help, but he ran away. I tried to ask Owl for help, but he only wanted to talk about my parents. I know that Fox tried to help me, and I showed him my foot, but he did not look at it. I told Tiger about my foot, but that only made him angrier. No one wants to help me."

"So, your foot is the problem?" asked Squirrel.

"Yes!" roared Crocodile. "I got a thorn stuck in it a few weeks ago, and I can't get it out. Why won't anyone help me?"

"They are too silly," said Squirrel. "Can I take a look?"

"Please!" shouted Crocodile.

Squirrel came down from his tree to take a look.

"Honey," he said.

"I thought that it would help if I dipped my foot in it," shouted Crocodile.

"I think that I see it. This might hurt a little. One, two, three!"

"Roar!" roared Crocodile.

"Got it," said Squirrel.

As soon as the thorn was out of his foot, Crocodile felt much better.

"I'm not really an angry crocodile," said Crocodile.

"Hey, anyone would be angry if they had a thorn stuck in their foot," said Squirrel.

"Thanks for helping me," said Crocodile.

"Any time," said Squirrel.

The two of them became best friends and enjoyed the rest of the honey together.

www.ingramcontent.com/pod-product-compliance
Lightning Source LLC
Chambersburg PA
CBHW081407080526
44589CB00016B/2494